Botha, Smuts and South Africa

Men and History

Collier Books ready or in preparation

BASIL WILLIAMS

BOTHA, SMUTS AND SOUTH AFRICA

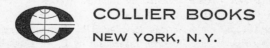
COLLIER BOOKS
NEW YORK, N.Y.

This Collier Books edition is published by arrangement with The Macmillan Company

Collier Books is a division of The Crowell-Collier Publishing Company

First Collier Books Edition 1962

First published in 1946
This title first appeared as a volume in the Teach Yourself History Series under the general editorship of A. L. Rowse.
Hecho en los E.E.U.U.
Printed in the United States of America

Contents

Preface

THIS BOOK has been a labour of love, prompted by a deep admiration of those two great men Botha and Smuts, and by a happy remembrance of four sojourns in South Africa.

I am specially grateful for talks, especially about General Smuts, with the late Deneys Reitz and his English friends Mr. and Mrs. Gillett.

B.W.

January, 1945

Chapter 1

The Setting of the Scene

LOUIS BOTHA WAS BORN in 1862 in Natal, and Jan Christiaan Smuts in 1870 in Cape Colony. Both therefore started life as British subjects. Botha's family, however, migrated to the Orange Free State in 1869 and thereafter Botha was never a British subject till 1902, whereas Smuts had renounced his British allegiance only seven years before that date.

The South Africa of the decade in which these two great figures of the British Commonwealth of Nations first saw the light was a very different South Africa from that which they grew up to know. It is true the boundaries of the four modern provinces of the Union—Cape Colony, Natal, the Orange Free State and the Transvaal—had been more or less definitely marked out, but these separate states were still very far from the goal of Union which they finally attained nearly half a century after Botha's birth. So far indeed were they apart that they all had divergent interests and policies, both with regard to one another and not least in their relations with the natives within their borders.

The original Dutch settlers at the Cape from 1652 onwards formed an essentially pastoral and to a less extent agricultural community of Boers—peasants—requiring vast farms of some 5000 acres on which to feed their flocks and herds, with relatively small patches for growing corn and vegetables for the family needs. An important accession to the Boer community came after the Revocation of the Edict of Nantes in 1685 with French Huguenot refugees, who brought with them a new industry, vine-growing and wine-making; but though their families have always retained their original French names, such as De la Rey, Marais, de Villiers, etc., they otherwise became hardly distinguishable in habits or language from their Boer neighbours. As the population increased the restricted settlement in the Cape Peninsula became too confined for its needs, with the result that families with all their possessions began to trek further north and east in search of new pastures so far scarcely occupied by wandering native tribes. After the final British occupation of the Cape in 1806 there was little increase in immigration until the 1820 settlement of discharged British soldiers with their families in the new Eastern province with headquarters at Port Elizabeth.

The Boers had always been difficult to control, even by their own governors; indeed, before the first British occupation in 1795 some of them had hived off and set up an independent government of their own out of reach of the Cape officials. With the final British occupation they found further grievances: English, which they did not understand, was made the only official language, and their own officials, field-cornets and magistrates were generally replaced by Englishmen. Another grievance came with English and Scottish missionaries, chiefly concerned with proselytizing the natives and with the defence of native interests against their Boer masters, who treated them as slaves. Even to-day Slagter's Nek, where in 1815 five Boers were hanged for rebellion in support of a man accused of cruelty to his Hottentot slave, is still remembered against the British. Finally in 1834 came the emancipation of the slaves within the British Empire, subject indeed to compensation, which, however, was not only inadequate originally, but also whittled away by heavy deductions payable to the agents entrusted with its distribution.

These and other grievances led to the Great Trek, or rather Treks, for there were several of them, beginning in 1835, of Boers dissatisfied with British rule, taking their families[1] and possessions in their great lumbering ox-wagons, and accompanied by their flocks and herds, northwards across the Orange River, so as to be beyond the reach of the alien government. Some settled between the Orange and Vaal rivers, others hived off still further north, beyond the Vaal, and others still eastwards into Natal. In these distant parts they set up little self-governing repub-

[1] One of these trek-Boer children was Paul Kruger, then a boy of ten.

lics, which, however, had very uneasy times with invading native tribes, Matabeles, Basutos, Zulus, far fiercer than their native neighbours at the Cape. At first the British Government, on the principle that once a British subject always a British subject, refused to recognize the independent governments set up by the trekkers; but, owing to the distances and the inadequate military forces at the Cape, could do little to enforce its authority. Natal, however, was in an exceptionable position: there was a good port—the modern Durban—which offered easy communication with India; and in fact a small English settlement had been established there before the Boers came in. Moreover the sparsely scattered Boer settlers were in constant danger from their fierce and well-trained neighbours in Zululand. Accordingly the British Government had much justification for asserting its authority and definitely annexing the territory in 1845. In Trans-Orangia, too, the trek-Boers had trouble with Basutos on the east and Griquas on the west and intestine quarrels among themselves. So great, indeed, were their difficulties that they made no serious opposition when, in 1848, the Governor of the Cape, Sir Harry Smith, extended British rule over this territory under the name of the Orange River Sovereignty. But it was symptomatic of the British Government's vacillating policy at this period that in 1854, only six years later, it abandoned the attempt at control beyond the Orange River and by the Bloemfontein Convention recognized the independence of the Orange Free State, as it was renamed. As for those Boers who had trekked further afield beyond the Vaal river, it was obvious from the first that they could not be controlled from Cape Town, nearly 1000 miles away: accordingly in 1852, by the Sand River Convention, the independence of the new Transvaal republic had been recognised. It must not be imagined, however, that it was simply owing to dissatisfaction with British rule that these expeditions to pastures new had been undertaken. Apart from the instance already quoted of Boers hiving off from their own government in 1795, as late as 1874 a party of Transvaal burghers, partly from restlessness, partly from dissatisfaction with the existing government, had trekked off to the inhospitable country in S.W. Africa south of the Portuguese border, where their few wretched descendants were discovered by Colonel Reitz in 1924.[2]

For a long time indeed the South African Republic of the Transvaal was too poverty-stricken and too much divided by factions to settle down satisfactorily. By 1877 the republic was almost bankrupt after an unsuccessful war with Sekukuni's native tribe in the Magaliesberg under an unpopular President, Burgers; and the intestine disputes had come to such a pass that a section of the burghers even welcomed the annexation of the country by the British agent, Sir Theophilus Shepstone. This annexation was in furtherance of the Colonial Secretary, Lord Carnarvon's, scheme of forming a confederation of the four South African states, Cape Colony and Natal with the Orange River and the Transvaal republics, a scheme which entirely failed partly owing to the tactlessness of Carnarvon's agents, but chiefly because none of the four states was then in favour of it. Unfortunately too, Shepstone failed to carry out his promise that the Transvaalers should retain full legislative powers, and they soon regretted their early acquiescence. Discontent increased under the rule of Shepstone and still more under that of his successor Sir Owen Lanyon: the defeat of the British troops at Isandhlwana by the neighbouring Zulus in 1879 only added fuel to the flame: and in December of that year the Boers, at a public meeting at Paardekraal, proclaimed the South African Republic once more, under the guidance of Kruger, Pretorius and Joubert. British troops not only failed to suppress the revolt but suffered the crushing defeat of Majuba in 1881. As a result Gladstone's Government in the following August formally acknowledged once more the Transvaal republic, subject, however, to British suzerainty, a claim, however, not specifically repeated in the succeeding convention of 1883. By this time both Botha, then aged 21, and even Smuts, at 13, were old enough to recognize the importance of this set-back to British influence in South Africa.

[2] See his *No Outspan*, 100–117.

Further extensions of British or Boer rule were still to come by the gradual absorption of outlying native tribes within their borders, and still more by the march of Rhodes's pioneer expedition into the interior of the continent up to the Zambesi in 1890 and later beyond that river. By that time, however, the South Africans were not left in undisputed control even of the south. The Portuguese, who had hitherto neglected their ancient establishments at Delagoa Bay, began to awaken to the importance of this territory on account of its port, the only one accessible to the Transvaal Boers, and later together with Beira useful for Rhodesia, and to reassert their almost dormant authority on the east, as well as their ancient claims to Angola on the west. But far more ominous for the security of the Cape was the gradual infiltration of Germans into South West Africa. In 1880 the British Government refused to extend protection to German traders there or to annex the country, as the Cape desired, and only agreed three years later to occupy Walvis Bay, the one good port in the territory. Accordingly, in 1884, Bismarck proclaimed a German protectorate over the remaining territory of South West Africa. In the following year, too, he established a protectorate over East African territory now known as Tanganyika, interrupting thereby Rhodes's design of an entirely British corridor from the Cape to Cairo.

To return to the Cape, still in 1870 and for many years to come the dominant factor in South Africa. Though Canada had attained self-government in 1845, the Cape had not yet reached beyond the stage of having a legislative assembly, able indeed to criticize, but not to control, the governor's nominated officials. This delay in obtaining responsible government was due not so much to unwillingness in Downing Street to grant it as to the Cape politicians' hesitation to accept it. The fact is that though the territory of the Cape was already large, its European population, according to the census of 1865, was only 181,000, intermingled with some 500,000 natives who contributed hardly anything to the colonial exchequer. But the main reason for the Cape's hesitation was due to the constant troubles on the frontiers with marauding natives, both within and without the colony, the suppression of which called for greater charges than the Cape felt able to supply from its own resources. For until the '70's the Cape was a relatively poor colony, depending almost entirely on its export trade to the mother-country of wool, hides and wine; there was a colonial debt of £1,420,000, then considered a large amount, two-thirds of which was due to Great Britain for advances made to meet past deficits.

Already, however, in the late sixties the first discoveries had been made of what soon appeared to be untold wealth in gold and diamonds. In 1867 gold was found at Tati in the great Bechuanaland corridor to the north, west of the Transvaal: and in 1869 the diamond later known as the Star of South Africa, which eventually changed hands for £25,000, was picked up in Griqualand, southwest of, if not actually within, the Free State border. One result of this discovery was a rush of diggers to Griqualand, which soon became an Alsatia dangerous to both claimants of the territory, the Cape and the Free State. The dispute as to ownership was referred to Keate, then governor of Natal, who, on the evidence before him, decided in favour of the British claim. In 1876, however, the evidence on which this decision was based was found to be questionable; but by that time the territory in dispute was peopled almost entirely by British subjects, and the Free State, unwilling to take over their government, accepted the sum of £90,000 as compensation for the erroneous decision. Four years later Griqualand West, hitherto governed as a Crown Colony, was transferred to the Cape.

But the excitement over the diamond fields of Kimberley and the surrounding district of Griqualand West was soon overshadowed by the rich deposits of gold found mainly in the Transvaal, at Pietersburg in 1870, at Lydenburg in 1872, at Barberton in 1882 and on the Witwatersrand in 1884. These discoveries, especially the last two, soon attracted vast crowds of prospectors and gold-miners to the Transvaal, which before and during the British occupation from 1877 to 1881 was almost a bankrupt state, and suddenly became potentially the richest in South

Africa. For Kruger, the new president of the Transvaal, took good care, by special taxation on the mines and by a monopoly of the dynamite essential for their working, to secure a large portion of their earnings for the benefit of the state.

The new wealth accruing to the Cape, largely from the increased trade brought about to supply the needs of the diamond diggers in Griqualand West, disposed the Cape Colonists to accept the higher status of responsible government with a ministry commanding the support of the electorate, which the home government had long been pressing upon them. From the outset, it should be noted, though the franchise was restricted by a fairly high property-tax, there was no colour bar. Natives attaining the necessary property qualification and a certain standard of literacy were allowed the full exercise of the franchise, though, as might be expected, at first few passed both tests. At first, too, it is notable, the English section of the European population alone took much interest in this new responsibility.

The fact is that in the early seventies the Boer farmers paid little attention to politics, being concerned almost exclusively with their pastoral and agricultural occupations, with looking after their native servants and with the daily reading of the Scriptures to their generally large families. In fact, they had little contact with the world outside their own domains, each of which amounted in extent to some 5000 acres, and it was the proud boast of most of these Boer farmers, each to be monarch of all he surveyed from his own farmhouse. Once a year, however, the farmers of each wide district did meet one another at the annual *Nachtmaal*—Holy Communion—celebrated at the principal, and sometimes the only village of their district, which was often many miles distant from most of the farms. Packing their families in their great ox-wagons, the farmers would congregate at the appointed place, camp round the village for the celebration of the *Nachtmaal* and for several days thereafter, making their purchases at the village store and above all congregating to discuss the affairs of the neighbourhood and rumours of the great world beyond. Their political interests, so far as they had any, were in fact concerned solely with the district within which they lived and annually met their neighbours; and they cared little for outside affairs as long as they were free to conduct their households and their farming operations as they pleased. Returned to their homes after these annual flittings, they resumed their patriarchal life, ruling their families and servants on the whole, with occasional exceptions, fairly and benevolently, while retaining the right of castigating those caught thieving or scamping their duties. In many of these scattered farms the only literature to be found was the family Bible, read and expounded by the head of the family, at the daily prayers. The only interference with the patriarchal and pastoral state of existence was on the eastern border, liable to raids from fierce border tribes, Galekas and Basutos, which necessitated the despatch of armed forces by the Cape Government. But even these raids did not at first stir up the Boer farmers to any consecutive interest in the central government, especially as the farmers there affected were mainly of English stock.

During the later seventies, however, came a notable awakening of the Cape Boers' interest in politics, due partly to their sympathy with the Transvaal Boers' revolt against the English Government's annexation of their country in 1877, and perhaps even more to the proselytizing work of two men, the Rev. S. J. du Toit, and Jan H. Hofmeyr, of an old Boer family. To both is due the recognition of the *Taal*, a form of Dutch general among the Boers, instead of the High Dutch of Holland, as a national language on equal terms with English. How successful these two pioneers were in arousing their Boer fellow-countrymen from their political lethargy is illustrated by the remark of Deneys Reitz, a shrewd observer, when he was travelling through Namaqualand, one of the most out-of-the way districts of the Cape, over half a century later: —"Politics is the ruling passion. For our farmers it takes the place of the theatres, cinemas and sport. It is the national pastime, like bull-fighting in Spain."[3]

[3] *Ibid.,* 35.

But in one important respect the two men had rather different aims; du Toit being frankly anti-British and for the closest co-operation between the Boers of the Cape and those who had trekked into the interior to escape from British rule and established independent governments north of the Orange and Vaal rivers; while Hofmeyr, though just as keen as du Toit in encouraging the Cape Boers to take an active part in politics, had no sympathy with du Toit's separatist aims. In the long run Hofmeyr carried his less provocative policy against du Toit. He even obtained control of the Afrikander Bond, founded by du Toit, eliminating therefrom its founder's more aggressive policy. For Hofmeyr, determined as he was to procure for the Boers the influence their numbers justified in the government, always kept it as his aim to consolidate the unity in South Africa of Boer and British interests— in fact, to create one South African nation in the same way as it has always been the aim of Canadian statesmen to merge the differences between French and English Canadians in the common interests of Canada as a whole. Hofmeyr indeed gave the best proof of his sincerity in advocating Dutch and English co-operation when in the eighties he was leader of a compact body of 32 Boer representatives, and, though refusing Rhodes's invitation to join his newly-formed ministry, gave it his support. In fact, ever since then there have always been sections of both Boer and English communities anxious to form a united party keen only on the well-being of the whole of South Africa.

Rhodes himself was entirely in accord with Hofmeyr in this policy, when he formed his ministry and for some time thereafter. Supported as he was by the Afrikander Bond as well as by a majority of the Cape members of British origin, he was able to carry out many useful measures, not the least being the Glen Grey Act, which, for the first time, gave to the Cape Natives an opportunity for exercising individual responsibility in the management of their own affairs.

The main difficulty in securing, if not real union, at any rate a working agreement between the Dutch and British elements in South Africa was undoubtedly the policy of President Kruger in regard to the gold-mining immigrants into the Transvaal, mostly of British origin, and contemptuously spoken of by the Boers as Uitlanders. They had no civic rights, were heavily taxed and were subject to a venal and bullying police force: Kruger even tried to kill the Cape railway traffic in goods to the Transvaal by prohibitive rates on the Transvaal stretch, and when the traders tried to circumvent this manoeuvre by derailing their goods at the Transvaal border and sending them by ox-wagons across the Vaal he closed the drifts on that river; on a protest, however, from the Colonial Secretary, Chamberlain, Kruger had to give way on this point. But the Uitlanders' grievances were still unredressed. Then came the blow to South African unity prepared by Rhodes himself, hitherto one of the chief advocates of such unity. He determined, on his own responsibility, and without informing even his own Cape cabinet, to solve the difficulty by the *coup de main* of Jameson's raid into the Transvaal. The raid, unbelievably ill-prepared, was a ghastly fiasco: it only strengthened Kruger's hand and necessitated Rhodes's resignation as Cape Prime Minister. But its worst consequence was that for many years it postponed any possibility of harmonious co-operation between the two sections of the South African white population.

Chapter 2

The Apprenticeship of Botha and Smuts

NO GREATER CONTRAST could well be imagined than that between the training of Botha and Smuts in their early days: and he would have been a bold man who had prophesied that they were destined to become not only the dearest of friends but also workers with identical aims in the same field of national politics.

The Botha family, according to one account, came to South Africa from Thuringia in the last quarter of the seventeenth century, though according to Lord Buxton, who no doubt obtained his information from Botha himself, they were of French Huguenot stock from Lorraine. But, whatever their origin, the Bothas had, like all these foreign immigrants, completely identified themselves in language and habits with the Boers of Dutch stock. Louis, born, as we have seen, in 1862, was the ninth child of the characteristically large Boer family of thirteen. In 1869 the family migrated from their farm, Onrust, near Greytown in Natal, to the Orange Free State, finally settling down on a farm near Vrede. Here Botha and his brothers and sisters had some rudimentary schooling from neighbouring teachers, but their main education consisted in learning—for the girls, household chores and simple cooking for the large family, for the boys, the South African farmer's craft on a large mixed farm of some 5000 acres, where sheep, cattle and horses were pastured and a comparatively small patch given up to raising corn, oats and vegetables for the family needs. Besides looking after the cattle and breaking in the horses, the boys were taught to shoot straight and get an eye for country. Here, too, Louis learned to understand and sympathize with the Kaffirs—first from the native servants on his father's farm—and to speak familiarly two of the chief native languages, Zulu and Sesuto; and not least to acquire his deep knowledge of his own Boer people in the rough and tumble of a large family ruled patriarchally by a notable father and mother, who became leaders of the neighbourhood.

As early as 1880, when he was only eighteen, he played a useful little part in the first Anglo-Boer War by cutting adrift all the boats and pontoons on his side of the Vaal, which were being used by English messengers to communicate with the troops on the Transvaal side. In the same year he was sent by his parents on his first independent adventure. With a bundle of food and clothing put up by his mother to strap on to his horse, at the beginning of winter he went off in charge of the family's sheep and cattle on the long month's trek across the Drakensberg range into the warm low-lying pastures on the border of Zululand. It was an adventure not without its perils, for Zululand in those days, owing to the exile of the paramount chief Cetewayo and Sir Garnet Wolseley's division of the country among several petty chiefs at odds with one another, was in constant unrest; and on one occasion at least Botha needed all his presence of mind to avert a serious peril. Usibepu, the most formidable of these petty chiefs, hot, it is said, from the murder of a missionary, suddenly appeared with his impi in Botha's camp and truculently demanded some of his beasts to feed his impi. Young Botha, who at the time had only a few cartridges left, quietly lighted his pipe and, after reproving the chief for his unceremonious approach, offered him one sheep on condition he and his impi cleared off at once, which they did forthwith. This was not the last time Botha had dealings with Usibepu.

These independent journeys with the family's flocks and herds, which he took off to the winter pastures over the border for four years in succession—added to his earlier training on the family farm—had already given Botha so much self-assurance and sense of responsibility that, on his father's death in 1884, he proposed to his brothers and sisters that he should be given the sole management of his father's estate, the annual proceeds of which he would, of course, divide fairly among them. But they would not hear of this proposal; accordingly Louis, determined to find scope for his special gifts, left the Free State and crossed over the border to his winter haunts in Zululand. It so happened that at this juncture there was a bitter struggle between two Zulu chiefs, Dinizulu, the son of Cetewayo, and Usibepu, with whom Botha had already had dealings; and Dinizulu had enlisted the help against his rival of Lukas Meyer, a Boer friend of Botha's, promising, if Usibepu were beaten, to hand over a Zululand district, later called Vryheid, to Meyer. Among other Boers who joined Meyer's small but efficient band was Botha; and, though Usibepu was far the more effective fighter among the Zulus, Dinizulu's party, reinforced by Meyer and Botha and their friends, overcame him. Accordingly, the district of Vryheid became a little Boer republic, independent for the time being of the Transvaal republic on its borders, with Botha's friend Lukas Meyer as its President.

Botha himself was promptly given responsible work in the organisation of the new republic, his first tasks being to survey the country, delimit the boundaries of the farms to be allotted to the Boers who had been fighting on Dinizulu's side, and lay out the new township of Vryheid. To Botha himself was allotted the farm Waterval, of about 3500 acres, close to Vryheid. Here was the home in which he began his married life; for in 1886 he took as his bride Annie, daughter of John Cheere Emmet, a collateral descendant of the famous Irish patriot, who had settled at Harrismith in the Orange Free State, and sister of one of Botha's co-adventurers in the fight against Usibepu. This proved an ideally happy marriage, for the two were in love with one another to the end, and to his business ability, gift of leadership and business acumen, she brought qualities somewhat lacking in him—a good education, a love of music and a sense of humour.

Two years after Botha's marriage the little republic of Vryheid was taken over by the Transvaal, and he very soon found thereby greater scope for his administrative talents. Field cornet of the district of Vryheid town in 1894, in the following year he was sent as a native commissioner to Swaziland, then under the protectorate of the Transvaal, and there did good work in suppressing some of the illicit liquor traffic which was doing untold harm to the natives. But efficient as he was in administration, his main interest, at this time, at any rate, was in his farming activities; and he was only too glad at the end of the year to return to his own home at Vryheid where, while resuming his post as field cornet of the district, he could devote himself to the improvement of his property. At the outbreak of the Boer War in 1899 he had increased his holdings in various parts of the Transvaal, such as Standerton and the bushveld, to 16000 acres, and possessed a flock of some 6000 sheep, including a dozen imported pedigree rams, 600 heads of cattle and 400 fine mares served by specially selected stallions. Nor was he averse to investment in other promising undertakings. In 1891 he had bought 1800 acres containing coal measures which, some twenty years later, he sold for £9000.

In spite of all these private activities he never lost sight of public affairs. In 1896, on news of the Jameson raid, he promptly mobilized the farmers of his field cornetcy and telegraphed to President Kruger, expressing the hope that "all rebels will be punished and made example of . . . Burghers were never more unanimous than now, and stand by the government as one man"; indeed, he is said to have urged that Jameson should be shot as a filibuster; Jameson himself hearing of this advice many years later remarked, so the story goes, "Yes, Botha was always right." But, though strongly supporting Kruger on this occasion, he was never in favour of Kruger's unenlightened methods of government, especially in regard to the Uitlanders; and in the presidential election of 1895 had supported the more liberal Joubert against Kruger. In 1897 he himself stood with his old chief, Lukas Meyer, for election to the Volksraad; both were elected, but Botha himself headed the poll. In the Volksraad, Botha, with Meyer and Joubert was generally opposed to Kruger's repressive policy against the Uitlanders and even proposed to cancel the iniquitous Nobel contract for dynamite, which bore so hardly on the mine industry, until he found that Kruger had bound the country to the contract and felt impelled to withdraw his opposition. But once the die was cast by the declaration of war against England in October, 1899, he was more than ready to do his duty by his own country.

Jan Christiaan Smuts, eight years Botha's junior, was the second son of a family of eight by his father's first marriage, with two more to come from a second marriage. Smut's parentage was more notable than Botha's, his father being a prosperous farmer of the rich Malmesbury district in Cape Colony, who was elected to the Cape Legislative Assembly, and his mother of an old Huguenot family, a woman of deep religious feeling and considerable culture. In his early days Smuts was of feeble health and a shy retiring lad, of little use on the farm, which his father had meant him to take over, his elder brother being destined for the office of predikant. It was not till he was ten or twelve years old (the authorities differ), when he was sent to a boarding school at Riebeek West, that for the first time, according to one of his biographers, he learned to read. But when he did start he became a voracious reader and was given special facilities by the headmaster, who soon realized his abilities and encouraged him in his new-found zeal for learning. At the age of sixteen he proved ripe for study at the Victoria College of Stellenbosch, first announcing his coming and asking for guidance in a touchingly naive letter to one of the professors. "Dear Sir," the letter begins, "Allow me the pleasure of your reading and answering these few lines. I intend coming to Stellenbosch in July next, and, having heard that you take an exceptionally great interest in the youth, I trust you will favour me by keeping your eye upon me and helping me with your kindly advice. Moreover, as I shall be a perfect stranger there, and, as you know, such a place, where a large puerile element exists, affords fair scope for moral, and, what is more important, religious temptation, which, if yielded to, will eclipse alike the expectations of my parents and the intentions of myself, a real friend will prove a lasting blessing for me. For of what use will a mind, enlarged and refined in all possible ways, be to me, if my religion be a deserted pilot, and morality a wreck?"[1]

At Stellenbosch he worked hard, and soon became so marked a student that when the great Rhodes came to address the college, he was chosen to return thanks for the students, and was noted by Rhodes as a young man of promise. But he still remained aloof from his fellows—with one exception. Among the women students was a Sibella Krige, six months younger than himself, with whom he soon found interests in common. Almost daily they would meet on their way to college; they studied Greek, German and botany together, talked of high philosophy, and in fact discovered one another as kindred spirits. After five years at Stellenbosch this self-reliant young man determined to go to Cambridge to study law, and, though he seems to have had little help from his parents, scraped together enough money—partly by borrowing from a Stellenbosch professor— to be able to enter as an undergraduate at Christ's College. Here, too, he was very much of a solitary; few, indeed, of his contemporaries seem to have met him. He himself later spoke of the debt he owed to Joseph Wolstenholme, a mathematical fellow of his college, who gave him much help in his reading. The only Cambridge contemporaries I have met who had spoken to Smuts in those days are Dr. G. P. Gooch and Archdeacon Lambert; but at any rate he attended the lectures of Henry Sidgwick on politics, and of that great humanist in law, Maitland, and worked to such purpose that he established a record by obtaining firsts in both parts of the Law Tripos in the same year. Then he went to the Middle Temple and was duly called to the bar. But law was not the only interest of this shy and solitary lawyer. In their walks and talks at Stellenbosch he and Sibella Krige, besides reading Goethe, had tackled Walt Whitman, in whom Smuts discovered the germ of his Holistic philosophy, and, during his odd moments at the Temple, wrote a book entitled *Walt Whitman, A Study in the Evolution of Personality,* expounding Whitman's view of the world, sent

[1] This letter is quoted in Millin, *General Smuts,* I, 12–14.

it out to Sibella Krige, who copied it out fair for him, and submitted it to a publisher. The publisher's reader was no less than George Meredith, who, while impressed by the book, thought it was not likely to attract enough readers to warrant publication. Then, in spite of brilliant prospects at the English bar, he decided to return to his native land. So far, except for his one confidant and companion, Sibella Krige, Smuts had been a solitary.

Settling at Cape Town Smuts began practising at the bar, but does not appear to have found many clients. The Cape lawyers and politicians have always been a genial crowd, accustomed to meet at their clubs, exchanging gossip and chaffing one another good-humouredly while treating one another to friendly drinks. In such a crowd Smuts was not much in his element, for he was still shy and reserved, very abstemious in his habits and too serious to join in the genial chaff. So he was not likely to attract many clients and in fact got little business at the Cape bar. However he was already an adept with his pen and to some extent made up for the dearth of briefs by journalism. Moreover, he found one influential friend in the leader of the Bond, Jan Hofmeyr, who was then allied with Rhodes, at that time premier of the Cape, and, though refusing to enter Rhodes's ministry, gave him powerful help in his endeavour to merge the Dutch and English comunities in a common programme for the benefit not only of Europeans but also of the natives. This was a policy which attracted Smuts from the very first and indeed, except for the interval of the Anglo-Boer War of 1899 to 1903, was always his main preoccupation in public affairs. Accordingly Hofmeyr recommended him to Rhodes as one likely to do good service for their common policy. Rhodes, indeed, perhaps hardly needed this advice, for he appears to have remembered the speech made by the lad in response to his own address at Stellenbosch in 1888, and invited him to make an electioneering speech on his behalf at Kimberley. No wonder Smuts, already inspired by the idea of a united South African nation, was attracted by the great man who seemed to have gone so far towards allaying, in the Cape at any rate, the differences between Boer and Briton, and accepted the invitation; and he made a brilliant speech, in face of a by no means entirely favourable audience, in favour of Rhodes's policy and attacking Kruger for his obstinate isolationism. Then came the Raid in December, 1895, and the revelation of Rhodes's complicity. To Smuts, no less than to the Hofmeyrs and Schreiners, Kriges and all the Dutch in South Africa, this came as a negation of all Rhodes's talks of and plans for the union of the races. "He alone," wrote Smuts, "could have put the copestone to the arch of South African unity. He spurned the ethical code. The man that defies morality defies mankind." Smuts's action was no less prompt than his words. Full of fight and fizzing with energy, he gave up his British allegiance and went north to carve out a new career in the Transvaal.[2]

On arriving at Johannesburg, besides giving law lectures and writing for the papers, he soon got a good practice at the bar, where there were then few who could rival his attainments. Thus he soon found himself well enough off to marry Sibella Krige, his one confidant in his shy retiring days at Stellenbosch, where the wedding took place on 1st May, 1897; and so began a happy marriage of a pair united in common interests in literature and above all in public spirit.

So successful had Smuts been at the Johannesburg bar and so eminently had he proved his staunchness for the Boer cause at this dividing of the ways between Boer and Briton, that even the old conservative Kruger had marked his ability; and in 1898 when Smuts was only twenty-eight, he was appointed State Attorney, second only in the ministry to the Secretary of State, Reitz. One of Smut's first actions as State Attorney was to clean up the Augean stable of the Johannesburg police, which had made itself especially obnoxious to the Uitlanders, by dismissing its

[2] In later years Smuts came to recognize, in spite of the Raid, that in his essential aim, Rhodes's was identical with his own for a union of both South African nations. For at the South African National Convention of 1908 Smuts confided to Fitzpatrick, "Oh, if we only had Rhodes at this Convention, how he would put all straight."

chief, whom he described as "a specially smart man, singularly unsuccessful in getting at criminals," especially in
the illicit liquor traffic and in the numerous disorderly
houses of Johannesburg; and a law was passed, in spite
even of Kruger, putting the detective force under the direct
personal control of the State Attorney. It may have been
on this occasion that Smuts, as he related in later days,
was told by Kruger: "Your whip hits too hard."

But even more serious matters than the disorderly state
of Johannesburg soon monopolised the attention of Kruger
and his government. Ever since the discovery of gold on
the Rand an ever-increasing stream of foreign—chiefly
British—immigrants, Uitlanders as the Boers called them,
had been pouring into the city and the gold-diggings on
the Rand. From the first the Boers, and not least Kruger
himself, were alarmed at this foreign invasion, which
threatened to swamp their comparatively small pastoral
community, and to introduce habits of luxury and extrava-
gance alien to their simple habits. But Kruger, realizing
that these Uitlanders had come to stay, had determined at
any rate to make them pay heavily for their accommoda-
tion. They were heavily taxed, not only directly, but also
through concessions given by the government to foreign
firms—not without a consideration to the State—for providing at exorbitant prices dynamite, etc., essential for
working the mines: at the same time they were refused
any say in the government of the country they were financ-
ing. For long their grievances found no redress, and after
the fiasco of Jameson's raid, they were in even worse
state. But in March, 1897, with the arrival of Milner as
Governor of the Cape and High Commissioner for South
Africa, they found a man prepared to stand up for what
he regarded as British rights. Milner, backed by the Colonial Secretary, Chamberlain, was determined not only to
remove their grievances, but also to assert in its most uncompromising form the suzerainty of the imperial factor
throughout South Africa. After much correspondence between Milner and Kruger, finally, at the end of May
1899, a conference was arranged at Bloemfontein between
Milner and the equally uncompromising old president.

Milner on his side required no promptings from his staff, who merely acted as his secretaries. Kruger, on the other hand, had been careful to take as one of his chief assistants his clever and ingenious young State Attorney, who, besides being fecund in devices, realized better than his chief that some concessions were necessary to avoid a war which might prove fatal to the Transvaal. Encouraged by sympathisers at the Cape, Smuts persuaded Kruger to make important concessions on the franchise for the Uitlanders, but he, no less than Kruger, was uncompromising about the suzerainty. However, Milner was not one to be content with any half-way house, and though a near approach was made to a satisfactory franchise, the conference broke down chiefly on the suzerainty question.

Smuts, however, still hoped that war might be avoided. He got into touch with Conyngham Greene, the British agent in the Transvaal, suggesting a more liberal franchise for the Uitlanders and admitting a nominal suzerainty for Great Britain, if it were never exercised. But this rather hole-and-corner negotiation never came to anything; for Kruger was not prepared to go as far as Smuts on the franchise question. Accordingly, Smuts, in his final letter to Greene, whittled away some of his original offer, and Milner insisted that any new approach from the Transvaal should come direct to him. Meanwhile, while Great Britain was still unprepared for war in South Africa, Kruger had been making his final preparations, and was waiting only for the first October rains, to bring on the grass for his mounted commandos, before proclaiming war. On 9th October he sent an ultimatum to England demanding that all British troops should be moved from the borders and reinforcements coming by sea sent back at once. On 11th October, 1899, hostilities began, with an invasion of Natal by Boer commandos. Thereupon Smuts wrote *A Century of Wrong*, a pamphlet recounting all England's so-called iniquities in South Africa, and ending with a peroration urging the unification of all South Africa under the Dutch Vierkleur flag. The pamphlet was forthwith issued by W. T. Stead in England; Smuts is said later to have regretted its bitter hostility to England.

Chapter 3

Botha and Smuts in the South African War

BOTHA, as we have seen, had been at least doubtful about the declaration of war by the Transvaal, but, the country once committed, he threw aside every doubt and was all for vigorous action. The war indeed soon proved the mettle of this quiet, wise man, then hardly more recognized, outside his own district of Vryheid, for what he was, than was Lincoln, "the prairie lawyer," before he first leaped into fame in his electioneering campaign against Douglas, the "pocket giant." As a simple field cornet Botha accompanied Lukas Meyer's commando for the invasion of Natal, but from the outset showed a dash and determination for aggressive action which soon brought him to the front, leading the first reconnoitring party across the Buffalo river and distinguishing himself in the battle of Dundee. Promotion soon came to him, for on 30th October, when Lukas Meyer fell sick, he was promoted to the rank of assistant-general, and shortly afterwards was put in command of the southern force investing Ladysmith. Here he was not content with the inactive policy of the Commandant-General Joubert, who proposed simply to sit round Ladysmith, blocking all communication for the garrison with the outside world until it was forced to surrender, but urged him, while leaving a blockading force round that town, to push on vigorously and possibly even reach the sea before the British reinforcements arrived. Yielding to Botha's pressing instances, Joubert crossed the Tugela river in November and swept round Estcourt in two columns. It is noteworthy that during this advance Botha ambushed an English armoured train near Chievely, and, meeting Mr. Winston Churchill unarmed and wandering about the line, took prisoner the future prime minister, and sent him up to his temporary prison at the high school in Pretoria. But British reinforcements were then beginning to arrive, and Joubert re-crossed the Tugela and, shortly afterwards falling sick, left Botha as the senior officer in command round Lady-smith.

Buller, on taking over command of the Natal forces at the end of November, decided to reach Ladysmith by a frontal attack on the Boer centre opposite Colenso. Botha, with that rare instinct for reading his opponent's mind, one of his most remarkable characteristics in the field, divined that Buller would choose this course, and accordingly, weakening his widely extended flanks, concentrated nearly all his strength on the centre. Here, on a semi-circle of hills facing the Tugela opposite Buller, he had dug himself in so securely and so unperceived by his enemy, that the advancing British troops were at his mercy. To make assurance doubly sure he gave orders that not a shot was to be fired until the enemy were actually crossing the Tugela. The Boers, however, when Long's guns came forward into action in an exposed position just south of the river, could no longer restrain themselves and, besides putting the battery out of action, so clearly revealed the strength of their position that Buller gave up his intended frontal attack. But had the Boer marksmen concealed their position a little longer, as Botha had instructed them, the victory would probably have been far more complete and a large portion of Buller's force put out of action.

Botha himself, after his defeat of Buller at Colenso, was all for an immediate advance on the British forces before Buller had time to readjust his forces. But, unfortunately for the Boers, Botha was not then unquestioned master of their military decisions, since he had not yet been appointed to the supreme command; while the various commandos besieging Ladysmith were too prone to act independently of one another. Nevertheless, when it came to actual fighting, Botha's clear vision and practical efficiency generally enabled him to impose his will on his colleagues. Thus at Tabanayama by his prompt call for volunteers to save the threatened right flank of the Boers he averted the danger. Again, in January, 1900, when a detachment of British troops had attained a commanding position on Spion Kop and many of the burghers had begun a panic-stricken retreat, Botha brought up guns to shell the British troops on the hill, rallied his burghers and launched a series of counter-attacks which finally dislodged the British. "It was," says one historian of this war, "Botha's persistent will to conquer that decided the issue." Again, in the last desperate fighting before Ladysmith in February, when Buller was working round the eastern flank, Botha forced him to retire from Vaalkranz, and telegraphed to Kruger, "With the help of the Lord, I expect that if only the spirit of the burghers keeps up as it did to-day, the enemy will suffer a great reverse." But after this Botha was constantly hampered by the less venturesome Meyer, who had returned to the front. After Buller's final success at Pieter's Hill on 27th February, Botha's attempt to rally the burghers was frustrated by Joubert himself, who gave the signal for a final retreat.

On the same day as Pieter's Hill, Cronje had surrendered to Roberts at Paardeberg, and a month later Joubert died. Thereupon Botha was appointed to succeed him as Commandant General of the Transvaal. Such an appointment was in itself an innovation, for Botha was then only thirty-eight, one of the youngest even of the commando leaders, and the Boers had as a rule an exaggerated respect for age. But Joubert had already realized his worth, and the still younger State Attorney, Smuts, is said to have finally persuaded Kruger to appoint him. At any rate he soon proved his fitness for the position. He was not one to tolerate the slack independence of the commandos, too inclined to dribble away home after a bout of fighting instead of maintaining the pressure at the front. One of his first actions was to send peremptory telegrams to the landrosts of the eastern districts ordering them to send back to the front all shirkers from the commandos: "act on this immediately," he concluded, "because every minute lost is in itself a wrong which you are doing to your country and kindred"; and he saw to it that his orders were obeyed. He also turned to better use the many foreign volunteers from Holland, France and Germany, hitherto looked on askance by the burghers, by enrolling them in a foreign legion divided into separate units, according to their respective nationalities and appointing in command of the legion the Comte de Villebois Mareuil, formerly a distinguished officer in the French army.

After the relief of Ladysmith by Buller on 27th February, 1900, and Robert's victory of Paardeberg on the following day, there was little left for Botha to do in Natal, whereas Roberts's march through the Free State towards Johannesburg and Pretoria threatened the very existence of the two Boer republics. So in May Botha took his newly reorganized commandos from Natal to the Free State. But with his force of only 10,000 as opposed to Roberts's 100,000, there was little he could do beyond delaying actions. At Doornkop on the outskirts of Johannesburg he made a gallant stand against odds, but could not prevent the occupation of the mining city and of the capital, Pretoria, by Roberts's troops. It is interesting to note that later, when the British were in full possession of Johannesburg, Smuts suggested a sudden *coup-de-main* by a force of 12,000—15,000 Boers to destroy all the mines with dynamite. Smuts then seems to have believed that the only object of the British was for the possession of the wealth of the goldfields, and expressed the view that "our plans, if carried out, would have meant a speedy conclusion of war," a view of Great Britain's reasons for going to war certainly erroneous. At any rate he never persuaded Botha to embark on such a hare-brained scheme.[1]

One last pitched battle, however, Botha had with the British shortly after the occupation of Pretoria. Kruger and most of his ministers, though abandoning the capital, had determined to carry on the government from a railway train, and were on their way eastwards by the line from Pretoria to Delagoa Bay. So, to prevent a premature success by the British advancing along the railway and so rendering the Boer Government's escape impossible, Botha decided to make a stand at Diamond Hill east of Pretoria; and, though he won no victory, by his delaying action facilitated his government's escape to the Portuguese border.

[1] Millin, *op. cit.*, I, 153.

So far Smuts, barring occasional visits to the Natal front to visit his friends fighting against Buller, had been kept at his work in Pretoria. But when Kruger and the rest of his ministry, mostly old men, left Pretoria for the railway, Smuts, only thirty years old and as vigorous as ever, remained behind, having made up his mind that the only thing left that he could do for his country was to fight in a commando. But first he saw to it that the government should be provided with funds for carrying on the war. Kruger had gone off in such a hurry that he had left the state treasure, consisting of bar gold valued at £500,000, in one of the Pretoria banks. When Smuts went to demand delivery of the gold, the bank manager absolutely refused to part with it, but Smuts, escorted by fifty policemen, soon overcame the manager's scruples and obtained the gold, which he forthwith sent down the line to Kruger's train; such a windfall was, of course, as nothing compared with the millions expended by Great Britain in the succeeding two years of war, but it served to some extent in providing equipment and food for the commandos that continued the fight for the next two years and more. Botha also was able to retrieve the £25,000 lodged in a bank in the name of the commandant-general for similar purposes.

Smuts at first sight seemed one of the last men likely to make a success of guerilla fighting. It is true that he had, on his return to South Africa from Cambridge, joined a company of volunteers at Stellenbosch. But so far he had appeared mainly as a student and as a clever and ingenious lawyer. He had never, except in his early days on his father's farm, seemed interested in anything but books, and in general company was shy and reserved. He had, no doubt, as State Attorney learned much of human nature, both good and bad, and could hold his own against men like the rascally police chief of Johannesburg, and even to some extent against men of Milner's calibre. But on commando he would have to be cheek-by-jowl mainly with men of little education except in farming work and uninterested in Smut's bent for literary and philosophic speculation. But to compensate for these drawbacks he had an eager determination to make a success of anything he undertook; and he shared with his fellow-burghers a passionate belief in his country's cause. Already, too, he was beginning to be known as "Slim Jannie," in a complimentary sense, for his ingenuity in dealing with rascally police officials, recalcitrant bank managers, and even, to some extent, with men of Milner's calibre. Such a man might well prove exceptionally useful in circumventing or harassing the somewhat lumbering British columns roaming about the countryside. These merits were quickly appreciated by the wise and understanding commandant-general, when Smuts applied to him for work on commando. Indeed, Botha seems at once to have recognised that in Smuts he had found an embryo leader in the hard struggle against overwhelming odds on which the Transvaal and the Free State were then embarking. So he accepted Smuts's offer and sent him to learn the guerila's craft under his friend de la Rey, the ablest and most successful commandant in the Western Transvaal.

The guerila war that was started after the final pitched battle at Diamond Hill lasted for all but two years. In the end, of course, the Boers—with forces far inferior in numbers, and with supplies limited to what they could find in their farms, which were being gradually bereft of inhabitants and produce by the columns of British troops, while the women and children were brought in to concentration camps—driven too, as they were, from pillar to post and gradually reduced by capture or losses in engagements—these fighting Boers were bound in the end to succumb to the overwhelming forces against them. But, suffering as they did, they earned the respect of their opponents and in the end secured a settlement which still kept the Boers as the predominant factor in South Africa. Among the Boer leaders of these guerila bands, while many inflicted serious reverses on the British troops, four stand out as most prominent, the Free Stater de Wet, and the Transvaalers Botha, de la Rey and Smuts.

In organising the guerila fighting Botha as a rule wisely entrusted the fighting in the various districts mainly to the commandos raised in those districts. There the men had their homes which they naturally wished to defend and also knew most of the by-ways from which they could make surprise attacks on the slow, heavily-moving English columns mostly confined to the well-marked roads or open country, or else evade them before they could be trapped by superior forces. Botha himself chiefly confined his own activities to the Eastern Transvaal, with which he was most familiar, but he managed, in spite of difficulties of communication, almost to the end of the war to keep in touch with the members of the two Boer Governments and the leaders of his scattered commandos. How wearing this guerilla warfare was to the British forces may be judged by an offer of Kitchener to meet Botha at Middleburg in February, 1901, to discuss terms of peace: the meeting took place, but without result, since Botha was not yet prepared to give up the independence of his people, a *sine qua non* on the British side. Kitchener, however, even at this meeting, was impressed by Botha's attitude, so much so that he wrote to the Secretary for War: "Botha is a quiet, capable man, and I have no doubt carries considerable weight with his burghers; he will be, I should think, of valuable assistance to the future government of the country in an official capacity."[2]

Six months later Kitchener, changing his tactics, tried threats instead of diplomacy to put an end to the tiresome war of which he was heartily sick, issuing a proclamation warning the Boers in the field that, if they had not surrendered by the 15th September, all their chief officers would be banished and the rank and file mulcted for the cost of keeping their wives and children in the concentration camps. Botha's answer to this threat was his own most spectacular expedition of the war. On the day after Kitchener's proclamation he issued orders to his commandos in the Western Transvaal. His plan was to invade Natal, unmolested hitherto by the Boers for over a year since the relief of Ladysmith, and not too securely guarded. On 17th September General Gough had a serious reverse at Blood River Poort; and though Botha failed in his immediate object of invading Natal, he attracted to his

[2] Quoted by Engelenberg, *General Louis Botha*, 66.

orbit several British columns hastily brought from other districts where they were much needed. These he evaded successfully, and then by magnificent marches—on one day covering thirty miles—suddenly swooped down on Benson's column, long the terror of the Eastern Transvaal —and almost annihilated it at Bakenlaagte on 30th October, 1901:—an effective reply to Kitchener's proclamation of 15th September.

By July, 1901, Smuts had learned enough of the guerilla art under de la Rey in the Western Transvaal to be chosen by Botha as commandant of a little band of 400 men to ride through the Free State and, after crossing the Orange River, to arouse the Dutch in Cape Colony itself. Taking little more in his saddle-bags than Kant's *Critique of Pure Reason* and a Greek *New Testament*, he set off gaily on the adventure.[3] During August he was involved in one of Kitchener's great drives in the Free State, but, after many hairbreadth escapes, reached the Orange River at the beginning of September, only to find almost every drift across the river guarded by French's forces in Cape Colony. Smuts, however, who always did his own reconnaissances himself, often alone[4] found one unguarded passage by which he led his men across. Henceforward for the rest of the war he remained in Cape Colony, eluding the English—even French himself—always pursued, often almost starving for want of food, but also occasionally surprising an English detachment and helping himself to English supplies and clothing. On one occasion he had got so far south as to be within sight of Port Elizabeth, and thence diverged westward to his own Malmesbury district, where he was met by a brother-in-law Krige, bringing him a large sum of money from Smuts's father. He gained a few recruits from the local Dutch, but not so many as he had hoped, since the English forces had commandeered most of the horses—and the Boer guerilla bands were compara-

---

[3] Hertzog, another Boer guerilla leader, told me that he took a Tacitus in his saddle-bags.

[4] On another of his daring reconnaissances, when he took three others with him, the party was ambushed by a British patrol, and Smuts alone survived to return to his commando.

tively helpless without horses, whereas the British could bring up their reinforcements by train. Occasional reinforcements however came to him from other Boer parties from the Free State, his most notable recruit being Deneys Reitz, son of a former President of the Orange Free State, who became the most lively chronicler of the adventure.[5] On one occasion French himself was within an ace of being captured by Smuts's little force, which had come to a halt one night by the railway line just as a train was approaching. They could easily have derailed the train, but Smuts forbade it, as it might contain women and children: in fact, as he subsequently learned, it contained only French and his staff on the way to reorganize his forces in the pursuit of Smuts's little commando. Finally Smuts, reinforced by more volunteers mainly from the two republics until his commando had increased to over 2000 men, made his way as far north as Ookiep in Namaqualand, where, after capturing a British fort, he was called away to discuss the final peace proposals at Vereeniging.

Smut's incursion into Cape Colony, in spite of all his difficulties, had been one of the most brilliant performances in the Boer War. With his own small force he had kept 8000—9000 British troops employed in defending British territory, and though he had won no great victories, he had at any rate kept his enemy guessing and to a considerable extent distracted. He had no hesitation in risking his own life, and in fact always insisted on doing his own reconnoitring and by his tact and personal courage kept his force, barring casualties, intact and enthusiastic to the end. After his years of active service in the open air, his very appearance had changed. When he first came to Johannesburg in 1896 he was described as "pale-faced, tremendously serious, with a hungry look, and seemingly taking no notice of what was around him"; now his closest relations did not recognise him with his new alertness and vigour, with "the breezes of the veld in his smile, its vast spaces in the sweep of his arm, its strength and unrelenting

[5] In his book *Commando*, for which Smuts wrote a preface.

spirit in the springiness of his rapid gait."[6] As to his military achievements, many years later, French, his chief adversary, presiding at a dinner to Smuts in London, said of him: "Smuts impressed me far more than any opponent I ever met, with his power as a great commander and leader of men."

A full account of the meeting of Free State and Transvaal delegates at Vereeniging is to be found in de Wet's *Three Years' War:* and a very moving account it is. Those most intent on continuing the war were chiefly from the Free State, notably President Steyn, ex-President Reitz and de Wet, though they at first found several from the Transvaal holding the same view. Against them was the majority of the Transvaal delegates and notably Botha and Smuts, who pointed to the almost complete exhaustion of their resources, the devastation of the country, the separation from their wives and children in the concentration camps and the comparative leniency of the English terms as almost irrefutable arguments for submission: the only alternative being the well-nigh complete annihilation of those who persisted in fighting against overwhelming odds. "We must save the nation" was the burden of both men's speeches to the delegates. "Terms might be secured now," said Botha, "terms which would save the language, customs and ideals of the people. The fatal thing would be to secure no terms at all and yet be forced to surrender. We are slipping back. We must save the nation by a permanent peace under which both Boer and British would be able to dwell here side by side."[7] With the same intent Smuts exposed with Thucydidean art the weakness of the national forces, praised their heroism and appealed to his countrymen to face realities and for the time being to yield "with the assured hope of attaining later," as he put it, "the glory of a nobler future, the light of a brighter day."

In settling details of the treaty both Botha and Smuts had several conferences with Milner and Kitchener, of

[6] N. Levi, *Jan Smuts,* 35 ff.
[7] The last words of this quotation come from E. V. Engelenberg, *General Louis Botha.*

whom the latter conceived a great admiration and liking for Botha, and by his frank talks with Smuts, in which he prophesied that within two years the Liberals would be in power in England and likely to grant a satisfactory constitution to the two new colonies of the Transvaal and the Orange River, greatly facilitated the Boers' acceptance of the British terms. At the final meeting of the Boer delegates on 31st May, 1902, when the British terms were presented for acceptance or rejection, the proceedings, as was usual with the Boers on such solemn occasions, were opened with prayer; and, after a few speeches, the treaty of peace as presented was finally accepted by fifty-four votes to six. Vice-President Burger of the Transvaal then spoke: "We are standing here at the grave of the two Republics. Much yet remains to be done . . . Let us not draw our hands back from the work which it is our duty to accomplish. Let us ask God to guide us, and to show us how we shall be enabled to keep our nation together. We must be ready to forgive and to forget whenever we meet our brethren. That part of the nation which has proved unfaithful[8] we must not reject." "Then this," so the chronicle ends,—"the last meeting of the two Republics, was closed with prayer."

On the British side, as soon as the treaty of Vereeniging was signed on 31st May, 1902, "We are good friends now," said Kitchener, as he shook hands with Botha, whom he had learned to respect as a formidable and straightforward antagonist, a sentiment entirely reciprocated by Botha about Kitchener himself, for whom he conceived a lasting affection.

[8] I.e., the National Scouts, Boers who had fought on the British side.

Chapter 4

From Responsible Government to Union

As SOON AS THE TREATY of Vereeniging had been formally completed, Botha called together his staff officers to thank them for their faithful services, concluding his speech with these prophetic words: "One consolation remains to all of you: you can now go and rest a little. As for me, my real work only begins at this hour. The day when rest will be mine will be the day when they lower me into the grave. The sacrifices we had to make were terrific, but we are going to see a Greater South Africa."[1] No prophecy could have been truer.

One of the first duties Botha imposed on himself was to seek relief for his own scattered people, most of whose houses had been destroyed, their livestock commandeered and their wives and children kept in concentration camps. It is true that £3,000,000 had been promised in the treaty by the British Government for restoring the burghers to their farms, but this was quite insufficient to make good their losses; so Botha, accompanied by De Wet and De la Rey, went off to Europe to raise funds from sympathisers in England and was particularly touched by his friendly and informal reception by King Edward and his wife; but neither in England nor on the continent, which he also visited, were the sums contributed to his fund for widows and orphans at all commensurate with his hopes.

On his return his immediate need was to find a new home, for his farm buildings at Waterval had been destroyed in the war; and the district of Vryheid, where they were, had been handed over to Natal at the peace. Accordingly Botha, who had made up his mind to remain a Transvaaler, bought a farm in the Standerton district, which he renamed Rusthof, Haven of Rest, gradually add-

[1] Engelenberg, *op. cit.*, 99.

ing to it out-lying properties until by 1912 he owned 11,000 acres. What Botha did not know about high-veld farming was not worth knowing, especially in stock-raising of sheep, horses and cattle. As he himself once remarked to a friend, "They may call me a soldier or a statesman— in reality I am a farmer and nothing else."[2] The story is told that on his visit to Europe in 1909 he was given a special permit to visit the French Government's merino stud farm and to purchase a few rams. Out of a flock of 150 he finally picked out three, which the manager declared to be the best on the farm: "Tell your Minister," he exclaimed, "that when I was notified of the coming of the famous Boer general, I never dreamt he was such an exceptionally clever sheep expert; on such occasions I always have our very best rams kept out;" and when Botha asked to make a selection of the two-year-olds, "Never!" exclaimed the worried manager, "I shall never be allowed to permit such a capable expert to take the pick of my two-year-olds. We have to keep them for our own use."[3] As a practical farmer, indeed, Botha was far ahead of the ordinary Boer farmers, who were quite content with the roughest unscientific farming which enabled them merely to provide little more, as a rule, than was necessary for their own households. In fact, much as he disliked Milner's methods of government in most respects, he made an exception in favour of his agricultural department, which did magnificent work in improving the Boers' happy-go-lucky system of farming.

But after his return from the disappointing visit to Europe he had little leisure at first for farming activities, for he had made up his mind that his primary duty was to help his own countrymen in their distress. Accordingly he took a house in Pretoria, where he was always accessible to those who came to him with grievances against the government and generous to those in special need. Though he and Smuts, who had resumed his practice at the bar, were offered places on Milner's nominated council to ad-

[2] *Ibid.*, 122.
[3] *Ibid.*, 186

vise the government, they both refused, as they disagreed with Milner's policy and felt that as outside critics they would be far more effective than as a minority in an unrepresentative assembly.

Smuts, the other outstanding figure among the Transvaal Boers, had after Vereeniging, during the last period of Milner's regime, at first given way to bitterness and despair as to the future of his country, especially when the employment of Chinese on the mines added another complication to the uneasy mixture of races in South Africa. His chief confidant in England was Miss Hobhouse who during the war had visited the concentration camps and done much to arouse indignation at home against the early defects of that system. Writing to her on the probable results of Milner's scheme of increasing the output of the mines by Chinese labour, he concluded: "I see the day coming when British South Africa will appeal to the Dutch to save them from the consequences of their insane policy of to-day. And I fear—I sometimes fear with an agony bitterer than death—that the Dutch will no more be there to save them or South Africa. For the Dutch too are being undermined and demoralised by disaster and despair, and God only knows how far this process will be allowed to go on."[4]

But this defeatist attitude happily proved only a passing mood, and Smuts was soon inspired by Botha to take an active part in his scheme for reviving the spirit of the Boers by starting a party to be named *Het Volk*, "The People," which, as its name implied, was to include the whole Boer people. The chief difficulty to be overcome was the unwillingness of the *Bitter-enders*, who had fought to the last, to have any association with *Hands-uppers*, Boers who had surrendered in earlier days and in many cases enlisted in the *National Scouts* organised by the British to fight against their own countrymen. But at the inaugural meeting of *Het Volk* in May, 1904, Botha made it plain at the outset that the composition of *Het Volk*

[4] Millin, *op. cit.*, I, 193-5. One of his bitter effusions was published without, I believe, his consent, and was answered by a bitter ode of Owen Seaman's in *Punch*.

must be as universal as its name: "Let us," he said, "put back the past so far that it no longer has any power to keep us apart. Less than a year ago we were in opposite camps—men of the same home passed each other without a handshake. To-night we are gathered in order to consider the fortunes of one and all. So mote it be. Let us do all we can to heal the breach, then we shall again become great. Let the names of 'Hands-upper' and 'National Scout' be excised from our vocabulary. The honour of the people is a thing too great and delicate to be tarnished by such stains."[5]. From this time forward *Het Volk* flourished under Botha's wise and tolerant guidance, aided by Smuts's resourcefulness and diplomatic ability[6] until in 1910 it became merged in the more comprehensive South African party, which by that time included also many of British stock; and even such obstinate extremists as Deneys Reitz, son of an ex-President of the Orange Free State, who had at first refused to take the oath of allegiance to Great Britain, "learned to see Botha's great vision of a united South African people, to whom the memories of the Boer War would mean no longer bitterness, but only the richness and inspiration of a spiritual experience. The loyalty of a Boer boy ripened into the broader liberty of the South African."[7]

The general election in England of 1905, which brought in the Liberals with an overwhelming majority was nowhere more enthusiastically acclaimed than in the Transvaal and the Orange River Colony, as it was then for a brief period called. The aim of Botha and Smuts was no mere half-way house of representative institutions, such as the abortive Lyttelton constitution proposed, without full responsible government by the people's chosen parliament: and there seemed to be a chance of obtaining full responsibility under the Liberals. So Smuts was sent over by *Het Volk* to explore the ground in England. He saw

[5] Engelenberg, 131–2.
[6] Recognising Smuts's diplomatic ability, the Boers chose him to expound their grievances to Chamberlain on his visit to South Africa in 1904.
[7] D. Reitz, *Commando*. (Preface by J. Smuts.)

several of the new ministers, none of whom gave him much satisfaction until he came to Campbell Bannerman himself. The Prime Minister asked him many searching questions about the past. Why had they not accepted Milner's offer of seats on the legislative council, or Lyttelton's Crown Colony government with seats in the legislature: questions to which Smuts answered that the one thing that could make the wheels run was self-government, giving his reasons at length. Smuts concludes his account of the interview. "I went on explaining, I could see Campbell Bannerman was listening sympathetically. Without being brilliant he was the sort of sane personality—large-hearted and honest—on whom people depend. He reminded me of Botha. He told me there was to be a cabinet meeting next day, and he added, 'Smuts, you have convinced me.'"[8] The story is well known of that cabinet meeting at which Campbell Bannerman, speaking against the view of all but two of his colleagues, by his "plain, kindly, simple utterance," which lasted only ten minutes, moved at least one member to tears and converted them all to the acceptance of the decision he had himself come to, to trust the enemies of barely four years ago, and grant the Transvaal and the Orange Free State, as it was once more to be entitled to call itself, as free and responsible a government as that of any of our dominions. "They gave us back," said Smuts, "in everything but name—our country. After four years! Has such a miracle of trust and magnanimity ever happened before? Only people like the English could do it. They make mistakes, but they are a big people." Botha, on the news of Campbell Bannerman's death in 1908, cabled to London his grief at the loss of "one of the Empire's wisest statesmen and one of the Transvaal's truest friends. In securing self-government for the new colonies he not only raised an imperishable monument to himself, but through the policy of trust he inspired the people of South Africa with a new feeling of hopefulness and co-operation. In making it possible for the two races to live and work together harmoniously, he had laid the foundation of a united South Africa."

[8] Millin, 213–14.

At the first elections under the new constitution *Het Volk* secured majorities in both the new colonies. But it was an encouraging feature of the election, in the Transvaal at any rate, that a certain number of English-speaking electors voted for *Het Volk* candidates and that some even of those elected on that side were of English origin. For it was the aim of both Botha and Smuts to merge these racial distinctions in a common patriotism for a South African nation. It was the aim, too, already proclaimed by a much chastened Rhodes as early as the end of 1900 when the war was thought to be all but ended: "You think," he said, to a meeting in Cape Town, "you have beaten the Dutch! But it is not so. The Dutch are not beaten; what is beaten is Krugerism, a corrupt and evil government, no more Dutch in essence than English. No! The Dutch are as vigorous and unconquered to-day as they have ever been; the country is still as much theirs as it is yours, and you will have to live and work with them hereafter as in the past. Remember *that* when you go back to your homes in the towns or in the up-country farms and villages, make your Dutch neighbours feel that the bitterness is past and that the need of co-operation is greater than ever. Teach your children to remember when they go to their village school that the little Dutch boys and girls they find sitting on the same benches with them are as much part of the South African nation as they are themselves, and that, as they learn the same lessons together now, so hereafter they must work together as comrades for a common object—the good of South Africa."[9]

With the majority secured at the polls by *Het Volk*, it seemed natural that Botha should be called upon to form a Ministry. At first indeed there had been an idea that Sir Richard Solomon, a Cape Colonial who had been Milner's Attorney-general, but had stood for Pretoria as a *Het Volk* candidate, might be chosen; but being defeated at the polls, he was out of the question. Smuts also was thought of by some of *Het Volk*, but he wisely stood aside for Botha. Writing to Merriman at the Cape he says: "I might

[9] Quoted in my *Cecil Rhodes,* 319–20; I was fortunate enough to hear the speech.

have been Premier, but considered that it would be a mistake to take precedence over Botha, who is really one of the first men South Africa has ever produced. If he had culture, as he has chivalry and commonsense, there would not be his equal in South Africa."[10] In fact Botha soon proved that actually there was not his equal in South Africa.

At the outset Botha showed his determination to make no racial distinctions in the composition of his small cabinet of six members. Besides being prime minister himself he also, most appropriately, took charge of the department of agriculture; Smuts, his *fidus Achates*, doubled the functions of colonial secretary and minister of education; of the four remaining ministers, two were of Dutch origin, but the two important offices of finance and public works were assigned to Hull and Solomon, both of British origin. Smuts indeed was justified in writing about a proposed testimonial to Botha. "The victory of the people's party at the polls is chiefly due to his never-flagging endeavours, which began on the day peace was proclaimed, in the cause of welding the inhabitants of the Transvaal into a compact, lasting organization; to his commonsense and well-considered counsel; to his moderate policy and his work for cordial race co-operation."[11]

As might have been expected, when self-government was established in the two former Boer states, in both of which, especially in the Free State, there was a large Boer majority, there was much pressure by these majorities to clear away lock, stock, and barrel, most of Milner's schemes and dismiss his imported officials, including especially the inner ring, the so-called "kindergarten," most of them first-rate young men. In the Free State, where Hertzog was minister of education, this policy was pursued with some vigour: but Botha in the Transvaal resolutely opposed such drastic measures, and in that was supported by Smuts. A few of the English officials resigned of their own accord, but all the best were willing to stay and were maintained in office; while most of Milner's

10 Engelenberg, 147.
11 *Ibid.*, 145.

schemes for developing industry, especially agriculture, were obviously too good to be scrapped. It is told of Botha that when a deputation of Boer farmers came to ask him to send back to England Milner's director of agriculture, F. B. Smith, later a distinguished fellow of Downing, he replied: "Wait till he has got rid of the cattle-plague, then I may see about it." In the same way he kept on all the other agricultural experts from overseas, who had been doing admirable work in encouraging the new scientific methods in veterinary science, agrostology, etc. Botha himself, of course, being one of the most expert farmers in South Africa, was fully entitled to judge; but even in this, and still more in other matters, he was not one to give his final decision without deep reflection. As one of his officials said: "When I first put up a proposal to him, he generally knew little about the matter, but would say: 'Well, I will think it over, and give you my decision.' When, a few days later, the decision came, it was invariably right."

The two questions which had loomed largest in the recent elections had been the importation of Chinese labour for the mines owing to a supposed dearth of native labour, and the education policy in the schools. As to the first Botha, with his extensive knowledge of native tribes and their habits, was convinced that with judicious and tactful treatment the native labourers would once more flock to the mines, and equally convinced that the introduction of another race with entirely alien habits into the already heterogeneous elements in South Africa was a cardinal error. But, unlike some of his Boer followers, who would at once have sent all the Chinese labourers packing, whatever effect that might have on the mines, he realised the importance to South Africa of the gold-mining industry, and was determined not to make too sudden a change which might disorganise it for an indefinite period. He therefore, though determined to get rid of the Chinese labourers in the long run, only gradually repatriated them until the new supplies of native labour which he was tapping had proved large enough to take their place entirely. Botha was well justified in his policy. Between January,

1907, and December, 1908, the natives on the mines had increased from 94,000 to 150,000 and by March, 1910, the last Chinese labourer had left South Africa.

Smut's chief achievement in this first and last ministry of the Transvaal as a self-governing unit of the British Empire was to elaborate a new educational policy. Under Milner's regime the old school buildings had been taken over as Crown property and a code passed which greatly improved the curriculum imposed by the former Boer government, with this serious defect that the medium of education was to be entirely English; with the result that the Boers had formed an Association of Christian National Education and started schools of their own to which they sent their own children wherever possible. Smuts's Education Act of 1907 wisely did away with this dual system and established free primary schools throughout the Transvaal, in which both languages, English and Dutch, were given equal rights according to the choice of the parents, thereby accustoming children of both nationalities, as Rhodes had foreshadowed, to come together at an early stage in the same schools. By this tolerant attitude Smuts antagonized many of the more bigoted Boer ministers of religion, and it may account for the charge sometimes brought against him of irreligion. At any rate in this reform, which was far more liberal than that instituted by Hertzog in the Free State, Smuts was warmly backed up by Botha, who, though no scholar and ignorant of the technical aspects of education, was all for good and cheap schools and above all for a system fair to English as well as Dutch: Botha indeed, used to say that the older generation could only be saved by tremendous efforts, and therefore everything should be done to educate the children at least.[12] In another respect Smuts was not so successful; for it fell to him to have the first dealings with a man and a problem that for more than ten years proved thorns in the flesh to himself and many others in the British Empire—Gandhi and the rights of Indian settlers in South Africa: but this problem may be more conveniently dealt with at a later stage.

[12] *Ibid.*, 158-9.

So far the grant of responsible government to the Transvaal had more than justified Campbell Bannerman's courageous decision to incorporate the two former Boer states as self-governing members of the British Empire. One of the first acts of the Botha government had been to present to the King, as a token of gratitude and goodwill, the great Cullinan diamond, the largest in the world, as an addition to the crown jewels. Within his first year, too, as premier, Botha had gone to the meeting of the Imperial Conference and there made his mark even among such experienced colleagues as Laurier from Canada, Deakin from Australia, and the former raider Jameson from Cape Colony; and he gained the affection of the British public by the many public speeches he was called upon to make during his brief sojourn in the country.

How sincere, too, was his determination to be a loyal member of the British Empire was illustrated by his consenting in 1908 to become a vice-president of the Champlain Tercentenary & Quebec Battlefields Association, as evidence of his right to take part in the consecration of the ground where the foundation of the British Empire was laid.

From the outset of their careers as responsible ministers of the crown both Botha and Smuts, as we have seen, had set before themselves as their main object to sink the differences between the two races, Boer and Briton, and weld them into one South African community intent only on the welfare of their common heritage. It was no easy task, for on both sides the rancour nurtured by the recent war was still alive. The British victors, in a minority in all the South African states except Natal, felt that, with the large Boer majorities in the two defeated states, the Transvaal and the Orange Free State, and with a preponderance of Boer voters even in Cape Colony, the fruits of victory had been thrown away; while the Boers on their side, especially in the Free State, were inclined to make up for their defeat in the field by their voting power in the elections. To Botha and Smuts it appeared that much of this racial antagonism might disappear if the four independent colonies could be merged into a comprehensive state concerned with the common well-being of the whole. There were other practical reasons for such a union. Each had its own customs policy, each its own railway system, to a great extent competing with those of the other three colonies, and each its own separate legal system and law courts. In fact, South Africa was over-governed, a cause, *inter alia,* of wasteful expenditure. Smuts, indeed, almost from the outset of responsible government in the Transvaal, had begun studying the question of federation or even complete union and comparing the different systems adopted for one of these solutions—in the Union of England and Scotland, the Dominion of Canada, and the more recent Commonwealth of Australia; and, no doubt also, the clumsy old system of the former Dutch Republic. Others had also been working along parallel lines, especially some of Milner's former "Kindergarten," as it was called, young enthusiasts such as Lionel Curtis, Robert Brand, Richard Feetham and Philip Kerr (Marquess of Lothian); while at the Cape men such as Merriman, Schreiner, Hofmeyr, and the new governor of the Transvaal, Lord Selborne, were turning their thoughts in the same direction. Indeed, as early as 1903 Milner had made a first attempt by his Intercolonial Council to deal with the common problems of railways and police for the two recently conquered Transvaal and Orange River colonies as a first stage towards closer co-operation throughout South Africa.

The question was first brought to a head in 1907 at a meeting of the Intercolonial Council, to which were now added Cape Colony and Natal. At this meeting the divergent interests of the four colonies were found so irreconcilable under existing circumstances that the only resolution adopted, on Smuts's motion, was that "the best interests and the permanent prosperity of South Africa was only to be secured by an early union, under the Crown of Great Britain." Accordingly in 1908 a National Convention was summoned of representatives from all the four colonies.[13] Meanwhile a battle royal had been going

[13] Delegates with a watching brief were also admitted from

on between the looser federationists and the advocates of the closest possible union. The most notable advocates of the federal solution were Hofmeyr and W. P. Schreiner at the Cape, neither of whom, however, was a member of the Convention, for Jan Hofmeyr always preferred to work behind the scenes, while Schreiner had accepted a brief for Dinizulu, the Zulu chief, whose trial for treason was impending, and so felt unable, for the time being, to accept other work.

The Transvaal in fact was the headquarters of the unitary movement. Botha and Smuts had fully made up their minds that the closest possible union would be the only effective solution of the fissiparous difficulties in the existing constitutions of the four existing colonies. "There is no alternative to Union except separatism. We must go the whole hog, one way or the other . . . What use is there in these tin-pot shows in South Africa . . . [We must] start a Union to rule the country from Table Bay to the Congo, and even beyond that"[14] was Smuts's ambitious scheme. To this end much good spade work was done by the so-called "Kindergarten" and their friends, both in the Transvaal and the Cape. Accordingly, when the National Convention was opened at Durban,[15] the Transvaal deputation, headed by Botha and Smuts, was the one best prepared to carry their views. Smuts indeed proved the most effective advocate of the unitary system, for he, in the words of the historian of the Convention, "had made a deep study of the question in all its details, and there seemed no aspect of the problem that he had not investigated with his habitual thoroughness . . . the clearness of his mind was fortunately accompanied by a corresponding lucidity of expression, and after the opening days there was no delegate that carried greater weight than General Smuts"; and of his speech in favour of the unitary system he says that it "made an impression that will never be

---

Southern Rhodesia, as it was then thought that colony might later join the Union.

[14] N. Levi, *op. cit.,* 122–4.

[15] Later the meetings were transferred to Cape Town.

South African National Convention 1908-9
Autographs of Delegates

effaced from the minds of those who heard it."[16] So convincing indeed was this speech that Jameson, hitherto a protagonist of the looser federal constitution, acknowledged that he had been convinced by Smut's arguments, and thenceforward supported the solution of complete unification.

But though thus early in the proceedings the crucial question of the form of union had been settled, there were still many difficulties to be overcome. At the outset Jameson, the ex-raider, had greatly facilitated a good understanding between the delegates by carrying his motion that English and the Taal[17] should both be regarded as official languages. Many other contentious questions arose, one of which, the question of the capital of the Union, aroused so much feeling among the different delegations that for a time it almost looked as if the whole scheme would have to be abandoned. It was in such difficulties that Botha stood out as the wise conciliator. He had not the wide knowledge or the dæmonic energy of Smuts, who, besides taking a notable part in the daily discussions, was often working half the night in preparing for the next meeting, while Botha preferred to relax with games of bridge in the evenings. But, when it came to momentous decisions, by his tact in dealing with his fellow-countrymen such as De la Rey and others, the respect in which he was held by them as well as by the British delegates, and his practical common sense in seizing upon the essential factor in a difficult situation, Botha was outstanding. It was largely due to him and Smuts that a solution was found for the difficulty about the Union capital. When, for example, De la Rey was proving obstinate about this question, Botha finally convinced him of the wisdom of the compromise finally adopted, telling him that "the Empire and the world were looking at them, and they would be eternally disgraced if they broke up the Convention on such an issue. What would be said of us; what would the King say of us at such a fiasco?" The final compromise, whereby

---

[16] Sir E. Walton, *Inner History of the National Convention of South Africa,* 1912.

[17] The form of Dutch used by the Boers in South Africa.

Pretoria was declared the seat of government, Cape Town the meeting place of the Union parliament and Bloemfontein the seat of the Supreme Court, was not in itself an ideal solution: but at any rate it was then the only means of preventing a breakdown of the whole negotiation. After the final sitting of the convention, the correspondent of *The Times* went to see Botha and found him "looking like a happy schoolboy" at the conclusion of their prolonged and anxious discussions.

Thus finally was accomplished, largely owing to the initiative and enthusiasm of Botha and Smuts, a union of the four governments in South Africa, which, as far back as the middle of the nineteenth century, had been the ultimate aim—to be attained by different methods no doubt —of governors like Harry Smith and Grey and Frere, secretaries of state such as Carnarvon and republican presidents such as Brand of the Free State and Kruger of the Transvaal. It came at the earliest moment that it could have come without what would have amounted to civil war; and it has been, on the whole, a most successful venture.

This successful issue of the National Convention's labours—though helped on by the harmonious relations between the delegates, in spite of differing opinions, and by valuable interventions on crucial matters by Merriman, Jameson, Farrar, and other delegates, and not least by the deeply respected chairman, Chief Justice De Villiers—was mainly due to the exhaustive preparation made for it by the Transvaal delegation and on critical points of difference, by the influence of its two leaders Botha and Smuts. Smuts indeed had been the thinker throughout with a complete scheme which he had carefully thought out and which he was equally successful in expounding. But when it came to almost insuperable difficulties such as the question of the capital, Botha was the great conciliator and guide. The habit of command which he had acquired in war he never abandoned, and all who approached him acknowledged it to be his right. He also had the saving gift of childlike simplicity. When the great work of the Convention was concluded, he rejoiced at its success like a boy at play. Childlike also was his loyalty to friends and causes, and his inability to understand what seemed disloyalty in others.[18]

Notable too is the letter he wrote to Asquith after the happy conclusion of the Convention:—"Now that the South African Bill has safely passed both Houses of Parliament and thereby the Union of the four self-governing Colonies in South Africa has practically become an established fact, I cannot refrain from congratulating you and the great party of which you are the leader upon the success which has followed your liberal policy in South Africa. . . . Only one thing is certain that only the liberal policy of your Government has made that Union possible. . . . Only after a policy of trust in the whole population of Transvaal and O.R.C. had taken place of one of coercion could we dream of the possibility of a Union of the Colonies, and above all of the two white races. My greatest regret is that one noble figure is missing—one man who should have lived to see the fruits of his work—the late Sir Henry Campbell Bannerman.[19]

[18] As special correspondent for *The Times* at the South African National Convention, I was privileged to know most of the delegates, notably that lovable Irishman, Sir Percy Fitzpatrick, of the Transvaal, and to learn much of the Convention's proceedings and difficulties.

[19] *Memoirs and Reflections* by the Earl of Oxford and Asquith I. 197.

Chapter 5

Union *versus* the Two Stream Policy

WHEN THE UNION Constitution, embodied in the South
Africa Act, had been passed by the Imperial Parliament
and assented to by the King on 20th September, 1909,
the question arose as to who should be the first prime
minister of the Union, and whether the first ministry
should be a coalition ministry of all parties or one con-
structed on purely party lines. To the post of prime minister Merriman, the Nestor among South African statesmen,
the last premier of the Cape and easily the greatest orator
in South Africa in the noble Gladstonian manner, had
considerable claims, even though these great merits were
to some extent offset by his being too great a master of
flouts and gibes. Undoubtedly, however, the chief reason
why the Governor General, Lord Gladstone, offered the
post to Botha rather than to Merriman was that in the
National Convention which had elaborated the new constitution, the Transvaal delegation, headed by Botha and
his lieutenant Smuts, had been the prime movers and the
most influential delegation. Botha accordingly accepted
the post of prime minister. In forming his ministry he at
first considered the scheme strongly urged by Jameson for
a coalition ministry composed of the best and most representative men chosen from all parties in the Union; but,
on consulting the leading members of his own South African party, he found them dead against it, nor did the chief
Cape politicians favour it. But, though he rejected the idea
of a non-party ministry, he was naturally careful to include in his cabinet representatives of each of the former
colonies; he could hardly do less in the recently formed
union of provinces, the respective interest of which had to
be carefully considered, at any rate until a more comprehensive South African feeling had come to maturity. As
before, his most trusted colleague was Smuts, to whom

were assigned no less than three portfolios, of Defence, Mines and Interior.[1] He himself besides being prime minister, also took, as before, the department of agriculture as his special province.

It is no derogation to several of the very able men included by Botha in his first South African Ministry that the only two members who really counted in it for general policy were Botha himself and his second in command, Smuts. Their partnership in politics which had begun almost immediately after the peace of Vereeniging, in 1902, thenceforward lasted unbroken till Botha's death. Now that they had united the four South African colonies, their great aim was to reconcile the two European races, Boer and Briton, and merge them in one united South African community with common aims and interests. As early as 1904, when bitter memories of the war were still vivid, Botha had declared, "Let us learn English, let the English learn Dutch, that will increase the chances of our forming a great nation";[2] and in 1912 as prime minister of the Union he declared his deliberate policy to be "the building up a united nation on non-racial lines." Later Lord Buxton, who as Governor General was in constant touch with Botha, and left a touching appreciation of him, thus described his aspirations,[3] "that the Omnipotent Father would embrace with unanimity all the white inhabitants of South Africa, so that one nation may arise from them fit to occupy a position of dignity among the nations of the world, where the name of Boer will be greeted with honour and applause."[4] And in this aspiration he found an enthusiastic supporter in Smuts, who, since the grant of self-government to the Transvaal, had entirely shed all the pessimistic views he had entertained directly after the peace of Vereeniging. Smuts indeed—"Jannie" as Botha called him affectionately—was far cleverer than his leader, and ready out of his own brain to find ingenious solutions

[1] The Ministry of the Interior corresponded in function with that of Colonial Secretary held by Smuts in the Transvaal.

[2] Engelenberg, *op. cit.*, 231.

[3] Buxton, *General Botha*, 12.

[4] *Ibid.*, 11.

of difficulties. Botha himself was the first to realize this; and, when an old Boer complained to him that Smuts had too much power in his cabinet, replied: "Old son, you people don't know Smuts yet. Our country is too young yet to play about with brains."[5] Moreover, except with Botha, he was more secretive in arriving at his decisions, which, though generally wise, were, owing to this secrecy, not so readily accepted by his opponents or sometimes even by his own party. In his long-drawn-out controversies with the diabolically ingenious Gandhi,[6] for example, he by no means always had the best of it, and, though he finally arrived at a working solution of the Indian difficulty, on several points he was obliged to climb down. On the other hand, in constructive schemes, such as the South African constitution, he always took a wide and tolerant view, which generally gained for them wide acceptance. Thus the two men were an ideal combination, as is well expressed by Botha's biographer:[7] "What Smuts was able to accomplish, thanks to his trained intellect, Botha achieved by sheer intuition. Botha and Smuts mutually felt the need of each other in public life. No petty jealousies ever vitiated their relations."

As Minister of the Interior, Smuts still had to tackle the thorny problem of Indian immigration, on which as Colonial Secretary of the Transvaal he had already had serious passages of arms with that redoubtable adversary, Gandhi. Indians had been admitted to the Transvaal during Kruger's regime, but only as hewers of wood and drawers of water, and were compelled, like the natives of South Africa, to live in separate locations and forbidden to own land: during the South African war many more, who had been doing hospital work for the British Army, found their way in, and, by the time responsible government was granted to the Transvaal, over 15,000 Indians had settled

[5] F. S. Crafford, Jan Smuts, 1944.

[6] Gandhi has always been a specially difficult man to deal with, largely because he never becomes bitter or angry in his controversies. When he was in prison in Johannesburg he made a pair of sandals which he presented to Smuts, who had put him there.

[7] Engelenberg, 332.

there, some having come direct from India and many more having trickled through from Natal, where they had at first been welcomed as cheap labourers on the sugar-plantations. The native inhabitants of South Africa were enough of a problem in themselves, but the added complication of another non-European race, mostly at a lower stage of civilization from Boers and British, was one that Smuts was determined, if possible, to remove. But, though Smuts himself was called "slim," he met in Gandhi one much slimmer than himself. Gandhi's chief points were first, that Indians as members of the British Empire, were entitled to migrate to other parts of that Empire, and secondly, that though it might be reasonable to impose restrictions on the free movement of coolies at a low level of civilization, it was outrageous that highly-educated Indians, like himself, should be forced to live in sordid locations where their freedom of movement was seriously restricted.[8] Gandhi by his agitation succeeded in securing the powerful support of the Indian Government against South Africa's restrictive policy; and, by the time he left South Africa in 1914, to embark on his campaign for *swaraj* (self government) in India itself, he had secured a notable alleviation of Indian grievances in South Africa.[9] He was indeed one of the very few men in whom Smuts more than met his match.

Smut's main achievement in the early days of the Union Government was his successful measure as Minister of Defence for the organisation of a national defence force. This task involved problems even more difficult than those concerned with education. Hitherto the British Colonies of the Cape and Natal had mainly depended for protection against native risings on volunteer organisations recruited

[8] When Gandhi, who had been called to the bar, first travelled from Durban to practice at Johannesburg, though armed with a first-class ticket, he was roughly hustled by the police into one of the carriages reserved for natives, mostly entirely uncivilized.

[9] It was not, however, till 1927, that an arrangement, made by Smuts with the Indian Government in 1924, was given legal force by an Act passed by the Hertzog Government. A useful summary of the Indian trouble is given by J. H. Hofmeyr in his *South Africa*, 180–4.

in South Africa; but, in the case of serious difficulties even against natives such as the Basutos, and still more in the Transvaal War of the 1880's and the South African War of 1899—1902, the main fighting had to be undertaken by troops from Great Britain, reinforced in the latter case by voluntary contingents from Canada, Australia and New Zealand. After the peace of Vereeniging the old Boer commando system of the Transvaal and the Free State was naturally in abeyance and a considerable body of imperial troops was retained in South Africa to meet any emergency. But, on the grant of self-government to the two Boer states and still more after the consummation of Union, it was obvious, both to the imperial government and to South Africa itself, that the Union itself must assume full responsibility for its own internal and external protection.

Thus one of the new government's most urgent problems was to raise a national South African force capable of defending the frontiers against any foreign enemy or, in case of serious civil disturbances, to supplement the police force of the Union. The old Boer system of raising commandos from the various districts of the Transvaal and Orange Free State had proved hardly a practical method of meeting the difficulty, for, though every able-bodied Boer was by law required, when summoned by his district field cornet, to present himself with his own horse and gun and provision for his own and his horse's upkeep, this system had been proved too haphazard to be satisfactory even in such a national war as that of 1899—1902. The full strength of a commando could never be relied upon, as its members were apt to take French leave to visit their families at home or on the plea of obtaining fresh provisions; and it required the authority of a Botha or a de Wet to enforce a better discipline among the men under them; and even they often found it impossible to prevent not infrequent leakages. Indeed Smuts, in a parliamentary debate, went so far as to suggest that, but for the Boers' lack of discipline and trained officers, the result of the South African War might have been different. For a national force to be ultimately responsible for good order throughout South Africa and, if need be, for defence against an external foe, it was obviously necessary to establish a disciplined national force not liable to evaporate at the moment of need. For this difficult task, especially difficult as being alien to the established customs of the Boer section of the community, Botha, relying on the practical resourcefulness and energy of Smuts, was well content to leave him in charge of the problem, especially as he could hand over to him suggestions he had received from Haldane, during a recent visit to England, about the reforms in the reorganisation of the British Army carried out by that great war minister.

As early as March, 1911, Smuts was able to outline to Parliament, his ideas of military reorganization, and in the following year presented his completed bill. "We want," he said, in an address to the staff college at Bloemfontein, "an organisation that shall not be Boer or English, but a South African Army." There was to be a nucleus permanent force of 20,000—25,000 men, made up chiefly from such former regiments as the Cape Mounted Rifles, the Mounted Police and the Cape Garrison Artillery, all voluntarily enlisted men. Next there was to be a Citizen Reserve, comprising men between the ages of twenty-one and forty-five who had voluntarily submitted to training; lastly there was to be a National Reserve, to be called out only on the gravest emergency and to comprise all citizens from seventeen to sixty. It was stipulated, however, that neither the permanent force nor the national reserve could be called out except for the defence of South Africa itself. He introduced his bill in a characteristically exhaustive speech, lasting two and a half hours and passed it without great difficulty. Naturally the scheme took some time to be elaborated in practice, and though one of the main considerations for its ready acceptance by the Boers was that the national force, when fully organised would render unnecessary the garrison of imperial troops that had been retained in South Africa since the peace of Vereeniging, few months had elapsed before these troops were found indispensable for the maintenance of order in the Union owing to a dangerous strike on the Rand in 1913. But in the following year, 1914, when an even more serious outbreak threatened life and property at Johannesburg, the government were able to quell it entirely with the defence force, and at the end of the same year, when every British regiment was needed at home to fight the Germans, the remaining regiments still in South Africa were sent back to England, leaving the Union entirely dependent on Smuts's new defence force for internal and external protection.[10]

Meanwhile Botha had been called upon to heal a serious breach in the harmony of his cabinet, on the all-important question of the relations between Boer and English citizens of the Union, especially in the Free State. In Cape Colony and the Transvaal, indeed, though the Dutch were in a majority, the citizens of British origin were numerous and influential, and, in those provinces of the Union, while it is true there were some irreconcilables on both sides, their influence was comparatively negligible; in Natal the white population was mainly of British origin, but on the whole this province worked well with the conciliatory policy of Botha and Smuts: the real difficulty was in the Orange Free State province. Here a remarkable change of attitude had taken place since the death of President Brand, who had kept his state in friendly relations with the Cape, and was by no means in agreement with Kruger's anti-English attitude in the Transvaal. But, after Brand's death in 1888, the two succeeding Presidents, Reitz and Steyn, were violently anti-British; and, both during and after the Boer War, some of the most prominent "bitter-enders" came from this state. For a long time after the peace of Vereeniging, among the leading Free Staters who at first refused to acknowledge British sovereignty, were ex-President Reitz and his sons.[11] Even among those who accepted the peace of Vereeniging,

[10] To be strictly accurate, the last British soldiers quartered in South Africa, for the defence of Table Bay, did not quit till 1921, a century and a quarter since we first established a garrison there.

[11] One of these sons was Deneys Reitz, who later became reconciled and was subsequently High Commissioner for South Africa in London.

many in the Free State would have nothing to do with Botha's and Smuts's conciliatory policy and aimed at continuing the rift between the two nationalities. The most prominent of these was Hertzog, Minister of Education of the Free State till the Union, and then included in Botha's South African ministry as Minister of Justice.

Though Hertzog had accepted office under Botha, who for his part was pledged to the reconciling policy of moulding into a South African nation both Boers and British, and so, as he put it, establishing "the gospel of lasting peace among the white races," Hertzog on the other side aimed at keeping the two races apart by what he called his "two-stream policy." For some time Hertzog, though outwardly polite to Botha at cabinet meetings, had been going about the country decrying the British connexion and emphasizing his own "two-stream policy" in opposition to the rest of his colleagues. He especially opposed any contribution from South Africa to the Royal Navy, though Botha had declared that "the cabinet recognised their responsibility to undertake the naval defence of South Africa, as they had done on land," asserting that he had the Dutch people behind him in loyalty to the Empire.

Hertzog was a cultivated, well-read man, with a considerable knowledge of the classics, an entertaining talker on non-political topics, a clever lawyer and an able debater. But he had an *idée fixe* about the necessity of keeping his own people, the Boers, uncontaminated by too close an identity of interests with the British section of the community, by his "two-stream policy" as he called it. Occasionally swayed by a less exclusive and more generous impulse, as, later, he was for a short time after Balfour's definition at the Imperial Conference of 1926 of the absolute freedom in unity of the British Empire's component parts, he was always apt to revert to his particularist attitude about his Boer fellow-countrymen. Botha and Smuts, as well as Hertzog, were good South Africans, but, as Olive Schreiner said of the last, "he had the hardness and narrowness of South African life." At any rate at an early stage of his official career in the first

Union cabinet, he began preaching his particularist "two-stream" doctrine, not so much at cabinet meetings, but at excited meetings of his own Boer fellow-countrymen in the countryside, decrying the British connexion, and doing his utmost to counteract the more generous policy of Botha and Smuts to unite in their common interests the two races, British and Boer, and so to create a South African, rather than a racially divided, community. In fact, Hertzog seemed to be doing all he could to exacerbate and perpetuate the differences between the two races.

Botha himself, when forming his ministry, had been very doubtful about offering a place in it to Hertzog, whose bitter anti-English attitude had been to some extent illustrated by his much less liberal education act in the Free State than that drawn up by Smuts for the Transvaal;[12] "When Hertzog thought to improve relations between the two races, as he caustically put it, 'by talk about the possible treachery of the British' he reminds me of a man on his honeymoon telling people what he would do if his wife proved unfaithful to him."[13] But he had been over-persuaded by Smuts to admit him to the cabinet. For a long time Botha, though himself convinced that "the true interests of South Africa are not, and need not be, in conflict with those of the Empire, from which we derive our free constitution," bore with the difficulties Hertzog was creating by his inflammatory speeches in the countryside. But finally, in 1912, after a speech from Hertzog denouncing two of the most prominent English members of the South African Parliament as "foreign adventurers," whereupon the only representative of Natal in the cabinet resigned, Botha declared that his choice was, either to work with Hertzog "and see the two white races of South Africa divided into two hostile camps, or to remain true to the principles of co-operation upon which party and government had been formed,"[14] and that he had no alternative but to call upon Hertzog, as the real source of

[12] See above, Chapter 4.
[13] H. Spender, *General Botha*, 334.
[14] L. E. Neame, *General Hertzog*, 137.

trouble in the cabinet, to resign. Hertzog characteristically refused to resign from a cabinet in which he was in a minority of one; so Botha felt that the only course left open was to resign himself on behalf of the whole cabinet. The Governor-General, Lord Gladstone, thereupon called on him to form a new cabinet, from which, of course, Hertzog was excluded. Botha himself, besides being Prime Minister, resumed his office of Minister of Agriculture, for which he was so well fitted; Smuts gave up his previous portfolios of Interior and Mines, but retained his post as Minister of Defence and was also charged with the Finance Ministry.

At the Treasury Smuts was not perhaps at his best in his budget speeches, in fact after one of them, when troubles at Johannesburg had made him for the time being a tired man, he suffered a defeat for one of his proposals. But as Minister of Defence he, in conjunction with Botha, had a signal success in overcoming two serious disturbances on the Rand. The first of these was in July, 1913, when the white miners came out on strike and created a dangerous situation by firing public buildings, and, what seemed even more serious, urging the native workers to come out on strike also and attack the white inhabitants of the city. Botha and Smuts at once came up to the threatened city and, as the new South African defence force had not yet had time to be effectively organized, they were obliged to call up contingents of the Imperial forces still in South Africa, to quell the rising. Thereupon for the time being a somewhat unsatisfactory truce—for it can be called no more—was made with the strike leaders.

Early in 1914 there was a far more serious strike with even more violent rioting, started by the railwaymen, which for a short time paralysed the railways, and supported by the Rand workers. For a time Johannesburg was almost in the power of the strikers. But this time the government was well-prepared. Martial law was proclaimed, but there was no need to call out the Imperial troops, for the defence force of the Union was then ready to take action. A commando of 1000 citizen soldiers was brought into Johannesburg and de la Rey from the west came up with another force and trained guns on the head-quarters of the strikers in the Trades Hall. In imminent danger of their lives Botha and Smuts went about, almost unguarded, through the city, getting into touch with the truculent leaders and finally, in view of the display of force, persuading them to call off the strike. But this time stern measures were taken with the chief fomenters of the disturbances, who were not let off so easily as in the previous year: for Smuts, apparently on his own responsibility alone, and without any judicial formalities, secretly sent off nine of the strike-leaders to Durban, where they were forcibly put on the *Umgeni* and deported to England before they had time to apply to the courts for a writ of *Habeas Corpus*.[15] Naturally this high-handed action was questioned not only in England, but also in the South African parliament, where the government introduced an Indemnity Bill to cover it. Smuts himself spoke for three and a half hours on the first day of the debate on the second reading and another two hours on the second day; and, though the second reading was carried, he had to face prolonged opposition on every clause of the bill in committee. Finally the bill was passed rather unwillingly by the South African parliament. In England, too, Smuts's high-handed action was seriously questioned by many who had hitherto given continued support to him and Botha.

It was fortunate that by 1914 Smuts's defence force had been fully organised for action, since with the opening of the "World War" with Germany in that year the British Government had to recall for action in Europe the remainder of its troops in South Africa. Fortunately, too, the Botha Government was able to assure the London cabinet that not only was it prepared to assume full responsibility for the defence of Union territories, but also to undertake the conquest of German South-West Africa, which otherwise might prove not only menacing to South Africa but also a danger to our command of the alterna-

[15] One of these men thus deported, as in the case of Gandhi, showed no animus against Smuts, and later became secretary of Smuts's political party.

tive route to India and our other eastern possessions. Accordingly orders were issued for the mobilisation of the defence force, to be directed by Botha himself, with Smuts as his second-in-command, for immediate action against the German colony.

But before carrying out their engagement to the Mother Country the two statesmen had to deal with a serious internal danger. It was characteristic of Botha's cautious and deliberate methods that, though he had forthwith assured the British Government that he would undertake the conquest of German South-West Africa, for some time he made no public announcement of his intentions. From the outset he had seen he would have to tread warily with his own people. Many of the South African Dutch who favoured the "two-stream" policy of Hertzog, especially in the Free State, and many even of Botha's own supporters in the Transvaal, besides a considerable section in Cape Colony, were disposed to take up the attitude that the war was none of their business and that South Africa should remain neutral. As early, however, as in 1911, when the Dutch paper *Volkstem* was putting forward a plea for the rights of the Dominions to be neutral in any war in which Great Britain was involved, Botha had declared that, according to constitutional laws affecting the Empire, such neutrality was unthinkable, and no enemy would respect it.[16]

Nevertheless, in 1914 he was soon faced with a serious revolt against his policy. Beyers himself, the commandant of the new burgher defence force, de Wet in the Free State and Maritz commanding the force on the German frontier, took up arms against the policy of active intervention in the war, some of them even in concert with the Germans. Botha's own feelings at this revolt of his own people, many of whom had recently been his trusted companions in arms against the English in the Boer War, and his equal determination to do his present duty as a member of the British Empire are plain from his answer to a deputation from Pretoria: "For myself I am willing to submit to any

16 Engelenberg, 281.

personal humiliation, if this is necessary, rather than take up arms against my own people, many of whom fought with me through the war. But I will not betray my trust and if, after I have tried every method of negotiating, they still refuse to come in, I will move out against them with the commandos that I know will stand by me:" and to the new Governor-General, Lord Buxton, he said: "It is my duty [to command the loyal forces], and it is the only thing for me to do. Beyers and de Wet are strong men and have a big following in the country. There is no one else I can put in my place just now, so I must go myself." Moreover he tried his best to avoid fratricidal bloodshed. "My orders," as he told Lord Buxton, "were that the rebels were to be scattered and captured: let the rebels fire first."[17] In words recalling President Lincoln's attitude to the South he said, "I consider the central idea pervading this struggle is the necessity that is upon us of proving that popular government is not an absurdity. We must settle this question now: whether in a free government the minority have the right to break up the government whenever they choose."[18] It was characteristic too of his determination to avoid the danger of renewing an Anglo-Boer racial conflict that the commandos numbering some 40,000 men he called out to suppress the rebellion were taken almost entirely from the Dutch districts. On 28th October with these loyal Dutch commandos, since the rebels would not give in, he smote Beyers's main force near Rustenberg so effectually that it never recovered cohesion, while Beyers himself, after wandering about with small detachments, was drowned in the Vaal on 8th November. In the same month Botha had defeated de Wet's force at Mushroom Valley, near Winburg, and de Wet himself was captured by a force under Coen Brits after a long flight through the western desert. By the end of February, 1915, the last rebels in the field had surrendered.

While Botha was thus disposing with considerable ease of the rebel forces in the field, Smuts, his *fidus Achates*,

---

[17] Lord Buxton, *op. cit.*, 78 ff.
[18] Neame, 174.

had been doing yeoman's service as Minister of Defence at Pretoria. When Beyers, before taking the field, had sent him a bitter letter denouncing Great Britain for over-looking the rights of small nations, disregarding treaties and employing barbarous methods in the South African War, Smuts sent him a truly devastating reply: "your bitter attack on Great Britain . . . is entirely baseless . . . your reference to barbarous acts during the South African War cannot justify the criminal devastation of Belgium, and can only be calculated to sow hatred and division among the people of South Africa. You forget to mention that since the South African War the British people gave South Africa her entire freedom under a constitution which makes it possible for us to realize our national ideals along our own lines, and which incidentally allows you to write a letter for which you would without doubt be liable in the German Empire to the supreme penalty . . . My conviction is that the people of South Africa will have a clearer perception of duty and honour than is to be de-duced from your letter and action."[19] To Smuts's work at headquarters during the rebellion, directing the movement of troops to reinforce this or that commando in the field, Botha paid this glowing tribute: "Nobody can appreciate sufficiently the great work General Smuts has done. It has been greater than any other man's throughout this un-happy period. He was at his post day and night. His brilliant intellect, his calm judgment, his undaunted cour-age have been assets of inestimable value to the Union in the hour of trial."[20] Smuts in his turn nobly acknowledged the even greater debt South Africa owed to his chief for the line he took in these critical months: "Few know," he said, "what Botha had gone through in the rebellion. He lost friendships of a lifetime, friendships he valued perhaps more than anything in life. But Botha's line remained absolutely consistent. No one else in South Africa could have stuck it out. You wanted a man for that, very broad-minded, large-hearted. People may say he went too far in that direction, but it is a policy that helped South Africa

[19] R. H. Kiernan, *General Smuts,* 73.
[20] N. Levi, *op. cit.,* 246.

over its worst stile. It was quite on the cards that after the Boer War the bad old policy would revive. Botha managed to wean the people of that."[21]

After the complete defeat of the rebels in the field Botha and Smuts showed a wise clemency. Only one man was condemned to be shot and that for a peculiarly dastardly and unnecessary murder of twelve loyalists: of the rest only the leaders had mild punishments, de Wet, one of the worst ringleaders, for example, though sentenced to six years' imprisonment, being released after a few months. In fact the two statesmen's chief aim was to wipe out the memory of this fratricidal incident as soon as possible; for, as Botha told Lord Buxton, "For myself, personally, the last three months have provided the saddest experience of my life. I can say the same for General Smuts. This is no time for exultation or recrimination. Remember we have to live together long after the war is ended."[22]

[21] *Ibid.*, 260.
[22] Buxton, 81.

Chapter 6

Botha and Smuts in the Great War

As SOON AS the rebellion had been quelled, Botha and Smuts resumed the task they had undertaken for the British Government, to take an active part against the Germans in South-West Africa. This German territory comprised an area of some 322,000 square miles, stretching from Portuguese Angola in the north to the Orange River on the south and from the sea to Bechuanaland on the east, with a narrow "Caprivi strip" on the north-west giving access to the Zambesi. Before its annexation by Bismarck in 1884 we had taken possession of Walvis Bay, the only good port on the Atlantic, leaving only two very inferior ports, Swakopmund, just north of Walvis Bay, and Luderitzbucht, further south, to the Germans. It was mostly an arid tract of territory, chiefly inhabited by wandering tribes, many of whom had been ruthlessly exterminated by a previous governor. The coast belt was almost uninhabitable, with hardly any water in the red-hot sand and burning rock; but the interior rose to an average height of 4,500 feet and had much potential wealth. When war was declared the regular armed forces of the Germans amounted to 2000 men, with 140 officers, under Colonel Heyderich; but in addition the settlers could provide some 7000 reservists; and there was a plentiful reserve of arms. Already, too, the Germans had established a system of railway communications, 1400 miles in length, with a line through the central plateau from Kalkfontein, near the southern border, to Tsameb, no great distance from Angola in the north, and connected by branch lines with Luderitzbucht in the south-west and Swakopmund in the north-west of the colony. Among the chief reasons why the British Government had asked Botha to seize the territory was that at the capital, Windhoek, in its centre, was a powerful wireless station, able to send messages to Berlin about the movements of our shipping along the west coast of Africa, and that at the beginning of the war the Germans had seized Walvis Bay, our only port on the west coast.

In this campaign also Botha took supreme command in the field, for, as he told the Governor General, "the plain fact of the situation is there is no one available to be placed in supreme command, except myself, who would have the full confidence of both sections, English and Dutch, of which [our troops] are composed."[1] But this time it was no longer necessary to confine himself almost entirely to Boer units of the national defence force, since both sections were at one in wishing to remove the German danger from South Africa. Already, before the rebellion, described in the last chapter, had begun, a force of 2000 under Colonel Beves had been sent by sea to seize Luderitzbucht with the ample provision, in view of the waterless, barren coast-country to be invaded, of 750,000 gallons of water and 500 tons of cold storage meat; the port had been taken without difficulty, and its 750 German inhabitants transferred to Cape Colony. While the rebellion lasted, operations in South-West Africa had been more or less at a standstill, though a small detachment of 257 had been cut off by the Germans in September, 1914, partly no doubt owing to the defection of Maritz, who was in command of the South African troops on the southern border of German South-West Africa. As early, however, as 8th February, 1915, the rebellion had been scotched and Botha was able to take stock himself of the position by visits to Luderitzbucht and Walvis Bay, which had already been recaptured from the Germans, and Swakopmund, which they had evacuated in January.

In actual manpower Botha had a great superiority over the Germans, with 40,000 Union troops all told, but in other respects the Germans had great advantages, with their command of a well-planned railway system enabling

[1] Buxton, *op. cit.*

them to concentrate troops rapidly on any threatened points, whereas, until the railways had been secured, Botha's forces had to march through arid deserts where, too, many of the existing waterholes had been carefully poisoned by the Germans. Accordingly, Botha's primary object was to obtain control of the railway lines as soon as possible. Having secured the principal bases on the coast, Swakopmund and Walvis Bay on the north and Luderitzbucht on the south, his plan was to advance along the railway from those points and close in on the enemy's main forces by a pincer movement. He himself took immediate command of the northern advance, while to Smuts was entrusted the direction of three converging forces up the main central line from the south. The three forces assigned to Smuts were Berrange's advancing from Kuruman on the east across a long stretch of the Kalahari desert, van Deventer's from south of the Orange River in the centre, and Mackenzie's on the west from the base already established at Luderitzbucht.

By the end of April, Smuts's three columns had, after some fighting and considerable hardship in the march by desert tracks, reached the central railway, as planned; and Smuts, after a visit to Botha in the north took directions for an advance up the railway simultaneously with the Commander-in-Chief's advance, north-east from Swakopmund. Smuts himself, after the advance up the central railway had been continued for some time by his three columns under Berrange, van Deventer and Mackenzie, had to return to Pretoria, where his presence was urgently needed at the Ministry of Defence in seeing to the prompt despatch of stores and equipment to the front; and the brunt of the fighting fell to Botha and his immediate command. By a magnificent march of forty miles without a halt through waterless country, Botha reached Karibib at the junction of the central and north-eastern railway lines, thus securing on 18th May the bloodless surrender of the capital, Windhoek, where the wireless station had already been destroyed by the Germans. Thereupon the German commander made the cool proposal that each side should be left in possession of the territory it was then holding, a proposal summarily rejected by Botha. Accordingly, after a month's halt at Windhoek for a needed rest and reorganisation of his troops, he continued his sweep up the central railway with his main body, until he reached the last junction, Otavi, with detachments under Myburgh and Brits ahead of him further north. Then at last, on 9th July, the German governor, Seitz, was forced to agree to the surrender of all German South-West Africa; but in other respects Botha's terms were lenient, as he felt, so he told the Governor-General, Lord Buxton, that "we should not do anything to hurt their pride unnecessarily; and you know how bitter such demands (at Vereeniging) on us made us feel."[2] The German troops, numbering by that time 204 officers and 3166 other ranks, were allowed to keep their arms for defence against the natives and to return to their farms. Of the 40,000 South African troops engaged, only 269 were killed and 263 wounded, so that this important conquest was lightly gained. It is notable that the British Navy gave useful assistance in this campaign by keeping the waters clear of mines, escorting Union troops to the disembarkation ports and even providing armoured motor-cars for the northern advance.

To Botha there was no vainglorious exultation at his victory. In a spirit of simple piety he thus addressed his men: "When you consider the hardships we met, the lack of water, the poisoned wells and how wonderfully we were spared, you must realise and believe God's hand protected us and it is due to His intervention we are safe to-day."[3] On the conclusion of negotiations, too, he issued to them this characteristic order: "Peace having been arranged in South-West Africa, all ranks of the Union forces in that territory are reminded that self-restraint, courtesy and consideration of the feelings of others on the part of the troops whose good fortune it is to be victors are essential." Throughout, too, Botha's attitude was all of a piece with this generous behaviour to a beaten foe: when, for example, after the torpedoing of the *Lusitania*, there were fierce anti-German riots in Johannesburg, he took the same

[2] *Ibid.*, 114.
[3] *Ibid.*, 40.

noble line: "Those johnnies," he declared, "are too funky to fight armed Germans, so they are bent upon ruining the unarmed ones, and wreaking their vengeance on poor women and children. I shall insist on protecting our German citizens."[4]

This successful campaign of a South African army, composed of British and Dutch fighting side by side, was characterised by Smuts, as Minister of Defence, in a general order to the troops, as "the first achievement of a united South African nation: both nations have combined all their best and most virile characteristics."[5] But, unfortunately, this healthier form of Union between the two races was not recognized so fully in the political field. The general election of 1915 was fought most bitterly, largely on racial lines. The antagonism to Smuts in some of the Dutch districts was especially virulent, and even Botha was hailed as "Judas, traitor, bloodhound, murderer," by some of his former supporters. Still, Botha's government retained a majority over the so-called Nationalists, while a strong party of Unionists, mostly British, in the main supported his policy.

At the outset of the war Botha's ministry, especially in view of the divided attitude of their own people in South Africa, had proposed to confine their military activity to the conquest of German South-West Africa, the most obvious danger-spot to the Union itself. But they very soon came to realise that the war could not be carried out in watertight compartments, and that a German victory in East Africa or even in Europe might threaten the independence of South Africa itself. Accordingly, when in 1915 the British Government appealed for further support from Botha's government, not only in East Africa but also in France, a ready response was made in allowing purely voluntary contingents to serve on both these fronts: and for the rest of the war South African troops gave valorous support to the Empire's efforts in Africa and in Europe.

[4] Engelenberg, *op. cit.*, 284.
[5] N. Levi, *op. cit.*, 256.

In German East Africa the need for help was especially pressing. This vast territory, co-terminous on the north with Kenya and Uganda, on the west with the Belgian Congo, Nyasaland and Northern Rhodesia, and on the south with Portuguese East Africa, was a standing menace to South Africa itself. At first the British Government appears to have thought that a force of 8000 Indian soldiers sent to Kenya and naval activity on the coast of German East Africa would at least enable us to hold our own. But unfortunately in September, 1914, H.M.S. *Pegasus* was sunk by the *Königsberg* at Zanzibar, and though in the following July the *Königsberg* in her turn was sunk, her crew and ten of her guns were safely landed and much needed rifles and ammunition were also brought ashore. Moreover, in their commander-in-chief here, von Lettow Vorbeck, the Germans had one of their ablest and most resourceful leaders, with his comparatively small force of some 3600 Europeans and 11000 Askaris, the finest native fighters in East Africa, and with sixty guns and eighty machine-guns at his disposal. By the end of 1915 the Germans had established themselves at Taveta within Kenya Colony itself and were threatening its main railway communication between Mombasa and the capital Nairobi.

By the beginning of 1916 reinforcements from South Africa were arriving in Kenya, and Smith Dorrien, famous for his gallant stand at Le Cateau, had been sent out to take command of operations in East Africa. But Smith Dorrien became so seriously ill on arrival at Cape Town that he had to be replaced. The British Government's first choice for the command had been Botha. He, however, felt that he could not abandon his post as Prime Minister, especially as communications with him in Kenya would be difficult, whereas in German South West Africa he was within comparatively easy reach of his own country. The next choice was Smuts, and, as South African troops were already there, Botha consented to his accepting the command.

Smuts lost no time in getting to work. Appointed commander-in-chief on 6th February, 1916, he arrived at

Mombasa on the 19th, and immediately went up country to make a personal reconnaisance of the enemy's position. As one who fought under both Botha and Smuts writes: "In German South-West Africa General Botha and in German East Africa General Smuts were either with, or immediately behind, and in closest touch with the fighting troops throughout the advances. The presence of their commander was looked for by the commandos, whose soldiers would have entirely misconstrued the action of a commander who conducted their operations remote from them."[6] Nay more, when, during the subsequent campaign, Smuts wished to make certain of the position, it is recorded that on at least two occasions with a few staff officers he went well ahead of his troops to reconnoitre, on the second occasion with only one Mauser pistol between the whole party, which might easily have been captured by half a dozen Askaris.[7] But, as in his incursion into Cape Colony during the Boer War, he seemed to have a charmed life.

During this preliminary reconnaissance he found the German invaders strongly posted on the eastern slopes of Mt. Kilimanjaro and holding the Ngulu gap between Kilimanjaro and the Same and Paré Mountains from Taveta in Kenya towards the Sangani River to the west. He at once decided that the first thing to be done was to clear the enemy out of the colony and then drive them southwards through their own territory. By a turning movement of detachments east and west of Kilimanjaro, synchronising with an attack on the enemy's force holding the Ngulu gap, he drove them entirely out of Kenya towards the Same and Paré Mountains south of the Ngulu gap. In connexion with this auspicious opening of Smuts's campaign, it is related that, when von Lettow Vorbeck met Smuts after the war, he asked him why he had posted van Deventer with a small force on a hill overlooking a German outpost. "Why," answered slim Jannie, "to induce

⁶ J. J. Collyer, *The South Africans with Smuts in German East Africa*, 74.
⁷ *Ibid., passim.*

you to bring up reinforcements there, so that I could circumvent you further west, as in fact occurred."

After this initial success he halted for a redistribution of his own forces. Van Deventer, the ablest of his generals, who had already done good work in South-West Africa, was given a semi-independent command with the task of guarding the western flank of Smuts's main advance. Starting from Moski, south of Mt. Kilimanjaro, van Deventer was to turn the Germans out of their strongly-held position at Kondoa Iranji and thence to push forward to Dodoma, on the central railway from Kigoma on Lake Tanganyika to Dar-es-Salaam, in co-operation with Belgian and British forces sweeping eastwards from the Belgian Congo, Uganda and Lake Tanganyika. Smuts himself, with the main force, proposed to clear the enemy out of the Paré and Usumbara Mountains south of the Ngulu gap, obtain command of the subsidiary railway from Morika to Tanga on the coast, and then to advance southwards to Morogoro, east of Dodoma, on the central railway, where van Deventer was to rejoin him.

Van Deventer, with one division, was the first to start on the southward march on 3rd April, 1916, reaching Kondoa Irangi on the 19th. Here he had to remain for three months, short of supplies and exposed to attacks from the enemy under the command of von Lettow Vorbeck himself; but he managed, with difficulty, to hold his own. Smuts, who had retained the other two divisions under his immediate command, had an even more arduous task. Repairs had to be made to the railway ending at Tanga, part of which was now in his hands, and a re-shuffling of his forces to be carried out; and it was not till 22nd May that he was able to advance. By the end of May he was master of the Paré Mountains, which the German missionaries on the spot had predicted it would take him two years to accomplish. When the War Office requested him to remove these German missionaries he protested on the ground that "it was an odious task which would be resented by Christians everywhere"; they were, he said, a civilising element, and, if these special missionaries must go, he urged that well-disposed missionaries should at once replace them, so that the good they had achieved should not be entirely lost.[8] On 2nd June, during a halt for supplies to come up, he undertook the cross-journey of 300 miles to Kondoa Irangi to discuss van Deventer's difficulties with him on the spot. Arriving there two days later, he found him hard pressed for adequate supplies and transport, and, after arranging for these defects to be remedied, was back on his own front by 10th June. By 12th June the Usumbara Mountains to the south of the Paré Mountains had been cleared, and Smuts established his headquarters at Handeni, some 100 miles north of his rendezvous with van Deventer on the main railway.

At Handeni, however, there had to be a long halt. The fall of torrential rains made the transport of much-needed supplies a slow and laborious business, while thirty-one per cent. of his troops, including Smuts himself, were for a time stricken with malaria and other tropical diseases in the pestilential climate. But during this dreary period of sickness and inaction, there was one brief ray of light, when Botha himself found time for a flying visit of two days to Smuts's headquarters, much to the delight of the South African troops and of Smuts himself, who was able to discuss plans and news of South Africa with his wise and experienced chief. Already, by 7th July, Smuts had secured the whole of the German northern railway, including the important port of Tanga, from Moshi to the sea; and now he began his drive down to the central railway, the only one still left to the Germans. By the end of July, van Deventer had reached Dodoma, due south of Kondoa Irangi, according to plan; less than a month later Smuts himself was established at Morogoro, the capital of German East Africa, further down the line; early in September he had captured Dar-es-Salaam, the last important sea-port, while the whole railway from Kigoma on the eastern bank of Lake Tanganyika to Dar-es-Salaam was in the hands of the imperial troops. By the end of September practically the whole coast from Mombasa to the Portuguese border was in our possession, so that the Ger-

[8] *Ibid.,* 135.

mans could no longer hope for any help from Europe.

Meanwhile von Lettow Vorbeck had taken up a position in the Uluguru Mountains just south of the railway with another detachment in the Mahenge range further to the south-west, almost the only fairly healthy parts left to him. Smuts, now co-operating with van Deventer, had cleared the Uluguru range by the end of September, but was never able to gain a complete victory over the main German forces, which, by the end of the war, though much attenuated, were still unbeaten. At this stage of the war Smuts realized that troops of European origin were too much subject to malaria and other wasting diseases to be of much further use, and began sending many of his South Africans home, relying more on Indian and West African troops who were less liable to these tropical diseases. He himself at the beginning of 1917 was needed in London for consultation with the imperial government, since Botha still felt he could not absent himself from South Africa: he had therefore to give up his East African command.

During one year in that pestilential and difficult country he had worked wonders, aided, it is true, in the later months of his command by contingents from Uganda, the Belgian Congo, Nyasaland and Northern Rhodesia. Von Lettow Vorbeck's force of 2700 Europeans and 12000 Askaris had by this time been reduced to 155 and 1168 respectively, and hardly any healthy parts of the colony were left to him; still he managed to give some trouble and maintain his tiny force in being till peace had been declared. It is characteristic of Smuts's appreciation of a gallant enemy that, hearing of the German's promotion to the Prussian *Ordre pour le mérite*, he at once sent him news of it by a flag of truce, "proof," as his adversary said, "of the mutual personal esteem and chivalry which existed throughout."[9] For his own men, Smuts was the ideal commander: he understood them, and they understood him and had immense confidence in him: he not only shared their dangers in the fore-front of the fighting,

[9] V. Lettow Vorbeck, *My Reminiscences in East Africa*, 1920, 170.

but took even greater risks than most of them by his adventurous scouting expeditions. Assuredly in his own conduct of these operations he cannot be accused of the errors of which he accused some British commanders: "You are prepared to lose a certain number of men, and you make your plans accordingly, but when a temporary check comes, you do not care to commit yourselves, and sometimes you do not follow up a victory fast enough . . . Tired, thirsty! there is no such thing when the success of a big operation trembles in the balance."[10]

Meanwhile Botha had not been having an easy time in his own country. Though he had won the election and was in most respects supported by the Unionist party, he was constantly faced with carping criticisms from Hertzog and his party, who while professing their loyalty to the Vereeniging settlement, made no secret of their preference for a purely republican form of government outside the Empire. In 1917 they opposed the grant of leave to Smuts to go over to England and in 1918 Botha's motion hoping that God would bring victory to Great Britain. They made great play with the difficulties that had arisen as to the price to be paid by Great Britain for the South African woolclip, on which nevertheless South African farmers eventually made large profits. At the conclusion of the war Hertzog renewed his claim for more freedom from the British Government for South Africa in a fiery speech declaring that "our blood had been poured out, our money wasted, our markets closed to forward the interests of Great Britain . . . our task master": "in fact," he concluded, "we are the spittoon of the Empire."[11] Hertzog and his friends even chartered a Dutch ship, refusing a passage offered them on a British man-of-war, and through the kind offices of Botha, then in Europe, had an interview with Lloyd George to press their views for a republican constitution no longer subject to Great Britain; but they obtained from him, as might have been expected, no satisfactory answer.

[10] Quoted by N. Levi, *op. cit.*, 290.
[11] L. E. Neame, *op. cit.*, 200–2.

Botha took this opposition of Hertzog and many of his old companions-in-arms very hardly. But, whatever his personal grief, he held staunchly to his oath of allegiance at Vereeniging, made all the more binding to him after Campbell Bannerman's generous gesture of trust, in the grant of responsible government so soon after the Boer War. In those hard years he missed the help of his dear friend Smuts, while Smuts was absent in East Africa or London, especially as he himself was often ailing with the seeds of the illness in him which was so soon to carry him off. In those hard years, however, it is good to feel he could always count on the Governor General, Lord Buxton's, sympathy. To him Botha's lovable nature, child-like sometimes in desponding moods, but always rising above his troubles when he saw his duty plain, was crystal clear. Buxton's *General Botha* is indeed a noble tribute to Botha as a man and a statesman.

Chapter 7

London, Pretoria and Versailles: Death of Botha

SMUTS ARRIVED in England on 17th March, 1917, expecting no doubt to return to his post in South Africa within a few weeks or at most a month or so. In fact, he remained in Europe for just on two years and a half. He had not indeed been in England for more than a few weeks before he showed what a valuable counsellor he would prove at the headquarters of the Empire, "full of courage," as he said of himself, and fertile in expedients to hasten on victory at a time when at best we seemed drifting to a stalemate. But his deepest conviction was expressed in the inscription he wrote on one of his photographs in this year: "Let us have faith that Right is Might, and in that Faith as to the end try to do our duty. J. C. Smuts."

Very soon after arriving in England he went on a tour of the French front, and on his return to London strongly urged a diversion of some of our troops either to Salonica or Palestine, whereupon he was offered the command of an army in Palestine. This he refused, as he had little confidence in the policy of Robertson, then chief of the staff at the War Office.[1] The Jews, however, grateful for his advocacy of their cause, subsequently named a strip in the valley of Zebulun *Ramat Jochanan Smuts*. In May he was entertained at a banquet in the Royal Gallery of the House of Lords, with Lord French, his old adversary in the Boer War, in the chair, and made a notable speech defining the British Empire as a misnomer, but rather as a community of states and nations, not forming one nation in itself, but a community "for consultation and co-operation, plus complete autonomy" for its constituent parts—anticipat-

[1] D. Lloyd George, *War Memoirs*, IV, 1830 ff.

ing in fact Balfour's famous definition of the Empire in 1926. In June he was invited to a seat in the War Cabinet and accepted it, subject to the proviso that he should not be called upon to deal with the purely internal affairs of Great Britain; even that stipulation, however, as will appear, was not strictly observed. So effective indeed were his speeches on imperial, and sometimes even on domestic affairs, that the well-known journalist, A. G. Gardiner, not inaptly dubbed him the "Orator for the Empire."

How pregnant with prophecies, later to be verified, his speeches often were, may be illustrated by his estimate of the consequences of the Russian revolution, at a time when most Englishmen deplored it, as marking the loss of an ally, and the fall of Russia into a quagmire from which she was never likely to escape. Very soon after the first appearance of Lenin, Smuts at the end of May, 1917, prophesied that "Russia . . . now seething in the revolutionary crisis . . . will concentrate itself, organise itself, discipline itself and then march again at the head of civilisation." Two months later, on the eve of the Brest-Litovsk negotiations, "If I were a German statesman," he said, "I would bear in mind the wise old Bismarckian policy and avoid making the Slav the future historic enemy of the Teuton," adding, even in the dark days of 1918, before the Germans had collapsed, "Let the Germans remember that Russia, now blind and turning the mill at Gaza may yet make the whole proud structure of German Imperialism topple down in ruin and confusion,"[2] words which some of our own statesmen might well have borne in mind.

Apart from his invigorating speeches about the Empire, his organising capacity had very early been recognised by Lloyd George and put to practical uses. Among other activities he was set to preside over the Committee for reorganising the Air Force: on his advice it was greatly increased, partly to deal more efficiently with the Zeppelin attacks on London; and, largely owing to his insistence, the R.A.F. was given an independent command, with a

[2] Quoted in *The Times*, 7-5-43.

status equal to that of the Army and Navy.[3] He also became a sort of handyman to the cabinet in going out to report on various fronts. Thus, he was sent out several times to France to hear Haig's views, to Egypt to discuss the Palestine and Mesopotamia operations with Allenby; and he accompanied Lloyd George to consult about the restoration of the Italian front after the disaster of Caporetto. He went also on two secret diplomatic missions to Switzerland to meet Mensdorff and an emissary of the Prime Minister Czernin, when Austria was toying with the idea of a separate peace, "dapplings for peace," which came to nothing, as the Austrians were too much bound to Germany to venture, when it came to the point, on a separate understanding. On both these missions, it is interesting to note, he was accompanied by his friend of the South African National Convention days, Philip Kerr (Marquess of Lothian).

Moreover, though he had originally stipulated that he should take no part in purely English politics, he even consented, at a critical stage of the war, to try his hand at stopping the Welsh miners' strike at Tonypandy. As he was leaving London, Lloyd George gave him just one word of advice: "Remember that my countrymen are great singers." So, when faced with an uproarious meeting of strikers apparently determined not to listen to him, Smuts, in a momentary pause in the din, shouted to them: "I come from far away, as you know. I do not belong to this country. I have come a long way to do my bit for this war and I am going to talk to you about this trouble. But I've heard that the Welsh are among the greatest singers in the world, and before I start I want you to sing to me some of the songs of your people." The response was immediate. Some started singing *The Land of our Fathers*. Thereupon the others to a man joined in the glorious singing: Smuts then had to speak for only a few minutes before the assemblage agreed to call off the strike.[4]

[3] D. Lloyd George, *op. cit.,* IV, 1863 ff.; R. H. Kiernan, *op. cit.,* 100–109.
[4] D. Lloyd George, III, 1373 ff.

When, in November, 1918, the armistice was signed, the last service given by Smuts as a member of the British ministry was to preside over the committee to deal with the question of demobilisation, but on 18th December he resigned so as to be able to take an independent line on the peace negotiations as one of the South African plenipotentiaries.

Lloyd George, who had ample opportunity of judging Smuts's work, said of him: "He is one of the most remarkable personalities of his time. He is that fine blend of intellect and sympathy which constitutes the understanding man. [Though a great fighting man], his sympathies were too broad to make of him a mere fighting man . . . He had rare and fine gifts of mind and heart. Of his practical contributions to our counsels during these trying years, it is difficult to speak too highly."[5]

Meanwhile Botha, during the long period when his faithful colleague was not there to help him with his buoyant optimism and fertility in expedients to overcome difficulties, was having a hard time in South Africa. He took especially to heart the persistent attacks of Hertzog and of so many of his old comrades in the South African war. They resented his loyalty to Great Britain and determination to rule South Africa in the common interest of the British as well as the Dutch section of the population. Of Botha's difficulties in 1917 Smuts from England said: "He is bearing a burden in South Africa which no other man can bear, and it is unfortunate in a sense that I have to take the place [in Europe] of my right honourable friend." To add to his difficulties Botha in that same year was seriously troubled, no doubt with the illness which ultimately proved fatal a few years later. Writing to a friend he said: "I was absolutely finished. I had given up hope entirely, thinking I should never see you people again; I felt that to go on living was an absolute impossibility"; but his spirit was great, and he ends the letter with these words of courage: "For a month now I have had no pain whatever . . . the heart is strong . . . blood-pressure

[5] D. Lloyd George, IV, 1763–4.

rather high, but better than it was; I walk up to nine miles a day and ride three hours . . . my mind is clear; I am full of ambition and schemes for a long life."[6]

In many respects he was more successful in dealing with his Boer compatriots than was Smuts with all his cleverness. Smuts, for example, was too impatient to deal with them in the old leisurely way to which they had been accustomed in Kruger's time, when they could come as a deputation to talk over some grievance with the old President and were allowed to sit on his stoep, smoking, drinking coffee and slowly discussing the matter for hours. Botha, on the other hand, favoured the old President's method. He would allow them to go through all their grievances, and, even if they did not obtain all they wanted, they felt some satisfaction in having been able to put their case at length. Botha, too, could smooth them down, even if he did not give way to them, by a joke or a happy retort that they could appreciate, as in the instance, already quoted,[7] of his answer to a deputation of angry Boer farmers demanding the dismissal of the English director of agriculture and the replacing of him by a Boer. By such tactful methods, indeed, Botha, in spite of his parliamentary difficulties, in which he was perhaps not at his best, or at any rate not so skilful in debate as Smuts, was often able to smooth away the opposition of his country Boers.

Botha, too, was fortunate in always being able to depend on the sympathy and good counsel of Lord Buxton, the Governor-General during the period of the war, and above all of his own beloved wife from the first days of his married life to the end. She, indeed, while never interfering with his work, made their successive homes in the Vryheid district and, after the war, in Pretoria and the farm at Nooitgedacht, the havens of rest and happiness that he needed. When, as so often happened during his life as prime minister, successively of the Transvaal and of South Africa, he had to be in Pretoria or Cape Town without

[6] Engelenberg, *op. cit.*, 332 ff.
[7] See above, Chapter 4.

her, every night his clerk had to get Standerton on the telephone: then Botha would take up the receiver and a lovely smile would come over his face: "Is that you, Annie?" and, after being assured she was well, he would enquire about the state of the farm: "Is the dam full of water?" "Yes." "Well, that's all right," and so to bed happy. It was indeed a true love match to the end. An English friend once happened to be calling on him at his hotel in London on an evening when General and Mrs. Botha were to dine at Buckingham Palace: after he had had some talk with Botha, Mrs. Botha came in, dressed for the occasion, and asked Botha, "Louis, do I look all right?" "Annie," he answered, "you look beautiful," and kissed her. Lord Buxton, in his little volume on *General Botha*, gives the most intimate and charming picture we have of the man. "I have known many big men," he writes, "Botha was the most human and the most lovable of them all. He was," he adds, "dignified, simple and natural, courteous and considerate: his stand was based on his natural sense of honour, duty and obligation. Essentially modest and unassuming, he hated personal quarrels, was a steadfast friend and a chivalrous enemy." His simple piety is well illustrated by his address to his men after the South-West African campaign, recorded by Lord Buxton, in which he attributes their safety and success to God's hand protecting them.[8] Above all, Botha, as a politician, was determined to do all he could to break down the barriers between the two races, English and Dutch, in South Africa. As the American statesman, Lansing, said of him after meeting him at Versailles: "A less broadminded and far-seeing statesman than the Transvaal general would have kept alive a spirit of revenge among his countrymen and counselled passive resistance to the British authorities, thus making amalgamation between the two nationalities a long and painful process. It would have conformed with the common conception of patriotism and the usual sentiment of the vanquished towards the victors, but it did not conform with General

[8] See above, Chapter 6.

Botha's views as to what was wise and practical . . . He did not permit vain regrets or false hopes to cloud his vision as to the future or to impair his sound common sense in dealing with new conditions resulting from the British victory . . . He accepted the fact of defeat with philosophic calmness and exerted all his influence in reconciling his fellow-countrymen to their new allegiance. Of the men I have met Botha was one of the greatest."[9] Even Hertzog, after Botha's death, was fain to admit that "the two races are learning more to appreciate what in the past they had regarded as each other's shortcomings." Of Smuts, Lansing took a less favourable view, saying that "he was often head in air and lost in thought . . . He had vivacity of mind which comes from a restless imagination and . . . impatience." But this restless imagination, even the impatience with obstacles, formed just the right complement to Botha's wise caution. At any rate they worked together to the same ends. Between these two great South Africans there was never a misunderstanding, still less a rift. Botha, speaking of this affectionate intimacy, would dilate on "the brilliant intellect, calm judgment, amazing energy, undaunted courage" of his beloved friend: what Smuts felt for Botha was expressed in the touching funeral oration he made when the final parting had come.

For the peace settlement at Versailles Botha had come to Europe as representative of South Africa together with Smuts, already on the spot. Smuts's last piece of work for the imperial government was to preside over the cabinet committee on demobilisation, but naturally, when appointed a South African plenipotentiary at Versailles, he resigned from the British cabinet. The great contribution that Smuts made to the peace conference was his earnest support of President Wilson's scheme for a League of Nations. In fact, Smuts has almost as much claim to the paternity of the scheme as Wilson himself, for it was he who drew up the original scheme of the charter which, with amendments added after discussion by the full conference, was finally adopted at Versailles. Unfortunately,

[9] Quoted in Engelenberg, 332, and Armstrong, *Grey Steel*, 250.

owing to the subsequent defection of America, Smuts proved wrong in his prophecy that "the League of Nations supplies the key to most of the new troubles . . . and it will bring America to our side in the politics of the future." At Versailles Botha used to sit next to Milner, since his South African days much mellowed as a statesman and one of the most helpful ministers in Lloyd George's cabinet. To Milner Botha during the peace proceedings said: "We have triumphed because justice has triumphed; but you must not in revenge destroy a nation . . . I and my colleague General Smuts alone here have fought a war and lost all, government, flag, all—and we remember. We knew the bitterness of defeat. [But] the English gave us peace without vengeance. They helped us to rise again, and that is why we stand by them again."[10] Smuts took the same line: "You may strip Germany of her colonies, reduce her armaments to a mere police force and her navy to that of a fifth-rate power; all the same in the end, if she feels herself unjustly treated in the peace of 1919, she will find means of exacting retribution from her conquerors."[11]

No wonder then that, when the treaty had been elaborated by the allies, and the Germans, without an opportunity of discussing its conditions, had no alternative but to sign what their enemies had decided, such a peremptory conclusion to their labours proved a bitter disappointment to Botha and Smuts. Maybe they judged the Germans by their own standards, and believed that, had they been given more generous terms, or at any rate been consulted, as had been the case at Vereeniging, the chances of a lasting peace would have been greater. Smuts indeed went so far as to refuse at first to sign the treaty, till he was urged by Botha not to stand aloof after all his hard work at Versailles, and reminded by him that without the treaty his own special clauses creating a League of Nations to prevent future wars, would fall to the ground: so Smuts finally gave his signature. But he afterwards wrote: "This Treaty is not the peace; it is the last echo of the war. It

[10] H. C. Armstrong, op. cit., 324–5.
[11] Millin, op. cit., II, 209 ff.

closes the war and armistice stage. The real peace must still come and it must be made by the Peoples." Botha wrote on his agenda paper for that day in Dutch: "God's justice will be meted out to every nation in His righteousness under the new sun. We shall persist in prayer in order that it may be done to mankind in Peace and Christian charity. To-day, the 31st May, 1902, comes back to me."

After the conclusion of the treaty Botha at once returned to South Africa. Smuts was much pressed to stay in England and he was sorely tempted to do so, but, as he said himself, "In the end I came back because of Botha. It was a choice between my loyalty to Botha and my missioner's feeling for the League. Almost at once I was left to do my work alone. It was good that I came back." So long had he been away that his two youngest children barely knew him: the two eldest, he found, thought he should not have signed the treaty.[12]

It was well that Smuts returned to South Africa, for, within a few weeks of his return, Botha himself, literally worn out by his incessant cares and labours in the field and the council-chamber, died on 27th August, 1919. His death was a calamity to South Africa, and hardly less so to the whole British Empire. *Loyal Devoir* might well have been his motto. Once having given his word for peace at Vereeniging, still more owing to the prompt trust reposed in him and his by the grant of self-government, no power in heaven or earth—the advice of old companions in arms or momentary political expedience—could move him from its implications. In his last speech, delivered at Bloemfontein only a week before he died, "he spoke," says Deneys Reitz, "in homely words of his desire for peace and unity."[13] His not infrequent visits to London had won him the respect and affection of Englishmen. His few brief speeches, always given in Dutch and rendered into English by an interpreter, breathed an air of sincerity and gallant courtesy, and above all of loyalty to his trust as a subject of the King that carried conviction of the man's

[12] *Ibid.*, 289–92; see p. 143, for Smuts's children.
[13] *No Outspan*, 27.

nobility of nature. In his own country the verdict of the immense majority of both English and Dutch was the same. True, some of those, like Hertzog, who had parted from him, thought he was too much wedded to the English connexion: but all felt him to be a simple, God-fearing man, with a lovable nature, not clever, but with the immense wisdom of the patient and the loving, such as he was. He was at his best, and certainly happiest, in his own prosperous and beautiful farm, where, with his beloved wife and family, he lived a patriarchal life, entertaining simply, and always the best of hosts.

Smuts, the colleague most unlike him in most ways, yet the one who knew and loved him best, said these words at his graveside: "He had no equal as a friend. We have worked together with a closeness seldom vouchsafed to friends. This entitles me to call him the greatest, cleanest, sweetest soul of all my days. Great in his lifetime, he was happy in his death. To his friend is left the bitter task of burying him and to defend his works, which were almost too heavy for him to perform."

Chapter 8

Smuts, Philosopher and Statesman

IT WAS SAID of Smuts: "With far greater intellectual power than Botha, with equal tenacity of purpose and indefatigable energy, with the same ardent patriotism, the younger statesman is not so well endowed with the gracious patience that made the late prime minister's person so winsome for all men." Smuts himself recognised this when he said: "I deal with administration, Botha deals with people." Later Smuts learned from hard experience some of Botha's gracious patience, but not till he had been tried in the wilderness of opposition for nine years, and then after close on seven years of co-operation with the man who first drove him from power in South Africa.

On Botha's death in 1919 Smuts naturally succeeded him as prime minister: but the results of the general election in 1920 showed that he could not carry on in the existing state of parties, for he mustered only forty supporters of his South African party against Hertzog's forty-five Nationalists, the rest of the House being composed of twenty-five Unionists (British), twenty-one Labour members and three Independents. First Smuts made a bid for support from Hertzog's party, but that fell through on the issue of a republican system, then Hertzog's *sine qua non*, whereas Smuts's attitude was that "if freedom could be gained only by way of a republic, I should be a republican. But our present status as a member of the Empire and of the League of Nations gives us complete freedom." Accordingly he then approached the Unionists, who in fact differed little from Smuts's policy, and agreed to be merged in his South African party. On this understanding he went to the country again in 1921, and obtained a comfortable majority of seventy-nine for his new South African party against Hertzog's forty-five and Labour's nine. It was unfortunate, however, for the prospects of the new ministry, composed of five Dutchmen and five Englishmen, that almost immediately after its formation Smuts himself was called to attend another Imperial Conference in England. At this conference Smuts was one of the first to warn the Empire about the dangers of Japan's jingoistic policy in the Pacific, which he regarded as a special menace to South African security. As usual, too, he was invited to resume his role as handyman of the Empire. He was asked to draft the King's speech for the opening session of the Ulster parliament, a speech which contained a message of peace not only to Ulster but also to the rest of Ireland, then seething with discontent. Smuts indeed was keen on Ireland as a whole obtaining Dominion status, but, from his own experience in South Africa, had no sympathy with de Valera's claim for an independent Irish republic; so when Lloyd George asked him to discuss matters with de Valera, then in hiding in Ireland, he at once agreed. Travelling as "Mr. Smith," he was taken to meet de Valera, Griffiths and Erskine Childers in their secret lair in Dublin; and, though he found de Valera and Childers opposed to any compromise on complete independence, Griffiths agreed to dominion status, as afterwards adopted. During this sojourn in England Smuts came very close to George V, and was much impressed by his "wisdom, modesty and unselfishness," adding that he had "the honour to be called his friend."

He returned to South Africa to find difficulties accumulating. The short boom which had followed the peace was succeeded by a period of intense depression. To make matters worse, in January, 1922, another strike broke out in Johannesburg, supported by some of the Nationalist party: there was a reign of terror in the city, and some of the leaders openly demanded a republic. So serious was the situation that Smuts himself, immediately after a speech in parliament, secretly went off by train from Cape Town to supervise measures on the spot. Some way from Johannesburg his train was brought to a standstill by demolitions on the line: but this did not deter him. Commandeering a motor car he drove on to the city, past crowds of strikers who even fired on him: he himself was not hit, but a tyre was burst and while it was being mended he remained cool and unruffled by the roadside surrounded by an angry mob. On arriving at Johannesburg he took personal command of the situation. Absolutely fearless at a time when many of the Rand and business magnates had fled to their country houses, he went about unarmed to address murderous crowds, escaping with his life solely by the respect his dauntless behaviour inspired; and, after calling in the citizen defence force, finally scotched the rebellion. When order had been restored he urged the mine-owners to show leniency to the strikers and reinstate most of the rank and file in their jobs.

In spite of this personal success, the economic condition in South Africa showed no sign of improvement, and, as usual in such circumstances, the government bore most of the blame for the depression, while Hertzog's prospects of obtaining power were rapidly improving. The prospect of a Hertzog government in the near future was especially unfortunate at this time for Smuts's cherished scheme for a greater South African state extending to the Zambezi and even beyond. It so happened that the first step in that direction seemed feasible in 1923, when Southern Rhodesia obtained responsible government. Smuts thereupon undertook a missionary journey to the new self-governing colony to persuade it to join the South African dominion as one of its provinces, instead of remaining isolated in the middle of Africa. But the Rhodesians remained deaf to his eloquent pleadings that they would not only gain in material prosperity, but also carry more weight in the counsels of the Empire than if they remained a comparatively small and isolated community in the middle of Africa. Had they been convinced that Smuts and his South African party would remain in power, they might possibly have listened more favourably to his pleading: but the growing strength of Hertzog's Nationalist party, which then cared little for the British connexion, seemed to them an irrefutable argument against any change of status. Since then the opportunity has never recurred.

In the same year Smuts, after attending another Imperial Conference in London, returned to find his majority in the South African parliament gradually dwindling from the original twenty-five to seven; and, after a crushing defeat at a by-election in the following spring, he dissolved parliament. At the ensuing general election Hertzog gained sixty-three seats against Smuts's fifty-three, and, on a promise to give up his claim to set up a republic, obtained the support of Labour's eighteen members. Smuts at once resigned and Hertzog formed a ministry, leaving Smuts in opposition.

The nine years of opposition that followed gave Smuts the time to deliver lectures, eagerly sought after in England, Scotland and America, and, in 1931, to preside over the British Association. Above all, also, he now at last found time to complete his book on *Holism and Evolution*, the philosophical system which was partly the outcome of his early talks and readings with Sibella Krige at Stellenbosch. He was able, too, to take more holidays in the open air, such as he had had very few opportunities of enjoying since Vereeniging. His first recorded jaunt was on his return from England in December, 1923, when he went with his dear friend Deneys Reitz on a trip to Zululand. On this journey, "his first real holiday for many years," Reitz records,[1] "he threw off the cares of state and we agreed to forget our political troubles for the time being; so we rode along gaily and he told us many interesting things about his work in England and Europe during the past years." On their way natives were warned of their approach by "bush-telegraph," and warriors appeared with tom-tom and war dances and presented them with a fat goat, of which they were supposed to take only the titbits, the rest going to the chief's retinue: at another place they were met by warriors of two hostile tribes, but fortunately, instead of a battle between them, they staged a combined war dance in Smuts's honour. Otherwise, when he could spare a few hours, Smuts's only physical relaxation was climbing difficult pitches—and there are many—on Table Mountain or in the Basuto

[1] D. Reitz, *op. cit.*, 60 ff.

Mountains. Even in his book on *Holism* he manages to bring in an allusion to his beloved pastime: "knowledge has given the key of power and mastery over the conditions which previously towered like an unscaleable mountain escarpment athwart its path of progress."[2] It is said that even to-day, when this youthful septuagenarian occasionally clears his brain by a stiff climb, the police escort attached to him in war-time, men much younger but less agile than himself, have considerable trouble in keeping up with their prime minister.

Hitherto Smuts had been known in England mainly for his work in the War Cabinet during the 1914–1918 war; but except for his address to the Tonypandy miners, he had had little opportunity of coming into touch with the general public, his work, as we have seen, having been mostly administrative and diplomatic. But from 1924 to 1933, being more of a freelance, he was able to respond to some of the numerous invitations sent him from England, Scotland and the United States to address learned societies and others on any topic he might choose. In 1929 he delivered the Rhodes Lectures at Oxford, dealing chiefly with South African and especially native questions in the Union, lectures which proved somewhat disappointing to ardent negrophilists. In 1931 he was elected president of the British Association for its centenary meetings held in London and at York and took his duties very seriously, for besides his inaugural address on *The Scientific World Picture of To-day*, dealing largely with his own theory of Holism, he also spoke at several of the sectional meetings; and in the same year he presided at the Clerk Maxwell Centenary celebrations at Cambridge. From America also he was overwhelmed with invitations to lecture. One enterprising lecture-agent proposed to him a lightning tour of the States, in which he was to deliver fifty lectures on any subjects he might choose, the remuneration offered being $500 for each lecture: he was also invited to give a course of lectures at Johns Hopkins University: both these offers he turned down. On the other

[2] J. C. Smuts, *Holism and Evolution*, 249.

hand he accepted with enthusiasm a proposal that he should make a tour of American and Canadian universities to address them on the League of Nations, the topic which he had almost more at heart than any other: it was a strenuous tour, but it probably did more than ever had been done before to arouse interest in the western continent on this subject. During this period, too, ever watchful of the Jewish problem in Palestine,[3] he made vigorous protests against the stringent regulations on their entry into what he had hoped would be a real national home for the Jews.

By 1934 he was once more in a South African ministry, nevertheless he managed in that year to fulfil a long-promised engagement to deliver the Rectorial Address, some time overdue, to the University of St. Andrews. This proved to be one of the most interesting of his speeches in Great Britain. The subject he chose was *Freedom*, taking as his text a favourite passage from Pericles's Funeral Oration, "Happiness is based on freedom and freedom on courage." At the start he put his Scottish audience in good humour by telling them of a talk with an old Hottentot shepherd at the time of the Majuba war, who, when asked who would win, replied "the English": "Are then the English the greatest nation in the world?" "No," was the old Hottentot's answer, "the Scots, of whom the English are very much afraid." Then drawing a parallel between the Scots and his own Boer countrymen as belonging, both of them, to small nations, while both took their full share in shouldering the burdens and promoting the welfare of their common Empire, he enlarged specially on the great civilizing and humanitarian work of their fellow-countryman, Livingstone, in his own continent. Passing on to the failure of Christian civilization in the Great War and the great chance missed for a better ordering of the future at the peace of Versailles, he then struck the more optimistic note of his central creed. In spite, he said, of past errors, "the world is still good to-day, it is a friendly world, built for heroism, but also for beauty, tenderness, mercy: that

[3] See above, Chapter 7.

is my ultimate *credo:* for there is no decadence, but more goodwill and good feeling than ever before": and that in spite of "the new tyranny (in Germany), disguised in attractive, patriotic colours, which is enticing youth everywhere into its service, a new tyranny, which in the words of Burke, was 'a weed which grows in all soils, and it is its nature to spread.' " As opposed to this new tyranny "to me the individual is basic to good world order. Individual freedom, individual independence of mind, individual participation in the difficult work of government seem to be the essential of all progress . . . Freedom is the most ineradicable craving of human nature; without it, peace, contentment and happiness, even manhood itself, are not possible. The fight for human freedom," he concluded, "is the supreme issue of the future, as it has always been in the past."

This last passage in his address at St. Andrews is specially interesting as introducing one of the main ideas underlying Smuts's book on *Holism and Evolution,* published in 1926, the result of half a life-time's thought since his first crude attempt to expound his philosophy of life in *Walt Whitman, a Study in the Evolution of Personality.*[4] Since that first attempt he had found further inspiration in the works of Whitehead, Lloyd Morgan and Adler, who said that in *Holism* "I see clearly described . . . the key of our science"; while Robert Bridges declared that his own *Testament of Beauty* was a poetical adumbration of an almost identical thesis.

In this mature volume Smuts sets out by defining "Holism" as "underlying the synthetic tendency in the universe, and the principle which makes for the origin and progress of wholes in the universe"; and by stating his aim as being "to account for the fundamental unity and continuity which underlie and connect Matter, Life and Mind," not merely in the human personality, but in varying degree throughout nature animate and inanimate. Well equipped for his task by his mastery of Darwin's theories

[4] See above, Chapter 2.

of natural selection, he had also studied to some purpose Einstein's concept of space and time in advance of Newton's discoveries, and he was familiar with the experiments made by Rutherford and others on the nature of the atom and of radio-activity in matter. Making full use of these recent advances in science, he claims that his theory of *wholes* or *holism* explains "the structure of matter and the arising, in, or through, matter of life and mind and personality," or, as he might have put it, *mens agitat molem.* To him indeed Personality is "the whole," expressed, not only in its highest, human aspect, but throughout nature, and always implying Freedom: "the function," as he puts it, "of the ideal of Freedom is to secure the inward self-determination of the personality, its riddance of all alien obstructive elements, and thus its perfection as a pure, radiant, transparent, homogeneous self-activity." Again, evolution to him is not merely a process, but is actually creative of "new materials and new forms from the synthesis of the new with the old materials."

An interesting parallel to Smuts's theory of *the whole* is to be found in that notable *Essay on the Dramatic Character of Sir John Falstaff* by Maurice Morgann (1777):—

"Bodies of all kinds, whether of metals, plants, or animals, are supposed to possess certain first principles of *being*, and to have an existence independent of the accidents, which form their magnitude or growth . . . It was not enough for Shakespeare to have formed his characters in the most perfect truth and coherence; it was further necessary that he should possess a wonderful facility of compressing, as it were, his own spirit into these images, and of giving animation to the forms. This was not done *from without;* he must have *felt* every varied situation, and have spoken through the organ he had formed. Such an intuitive comprehension of things and such a facility, must unite to form a Shakespeare. The reader will not now be surprised if I affirm that those characters in Shakespeare, which are seen only in part, are yet capable of being unfolded and understood as a whole; every part being in fact relative, and inferring all the rest . . . If the characters of

Shakespeare are thus *whole*, and as it were original, whilst those of all other writers are mere imitation, it may be fit to consider them rather as Historic than Dramatic beings; and, when occasion requires, to account for their conduct from the *whole* of charcter, from general principles, from latent motives, and from policies not avowed."

Professor A. D. Ritchie's view of Smuts's theory, which I am allowed to quote, is that "What seems to me the most interesting part of his theory is that it is an attempt to mediate between the view that what is new and emergent comes from without by sheer magic and the view that it is imposed from without by a transcendent Creator. The second view precludes any attempt at a scientific account by introducing something of which science itself is not cognisant. The first seems scientifically absurd. Holism is an attempt at a third line of approach."

Whether one accepts Smuts's views on the nature of man and the universe generally or not, at any rate there are moving passages in this book which not only stimulate thought but also give a noble and encouraging stimulus to human endeavour.

Take this passage in which he imagines a universe without mind: "It would have gone on sublimely unconscious of itself. It would have had no soul or souls; it would have harboured no passionate exaltations; no poignant regrets or bitter sorrows would have disturbed its profound peace. For it, neither the great lights nor the deep shadows. Truth, beauty and goodness would have been there, but unknown, unseen, unloved. [With Mind has come] sin and sorrow, faith and love, the great vision of knowledge, and the conscious effort to master all hampering conditions and to work out the great redemption. Purpose marks the liberation of Mind from the domination of circumstances and indicates its free creative activity from the trammels of the present and the past";—or this noble passage in his last chapter:—

"This is a universe of whole-making, not of soul-making only . . . Wholeness or the holistic character of Nature . . . has its friendly intimate influences and its subtle appeal to all the wholes in Nature and especially to the spiritual in us. For the overwrought mind there is no peace like Nature's, for the wounded spirit there is no healing like hers. There are indeed times when human companionship becomes unbearable, and we fly to Nature for that silent sympathy and communion spent under the open African sky . . . The intimate *rapport* with Nature is one of the most precious things in life. Nature is indeed very close to us, sometimes closer than hands and feet, of which in truth she is but the extension. The emotional appeal of Nature is tremendous, sometimes more than one can bear. . . .

"Everywhere I have seen men search and struggle for the Good with grim determination and earnestness, and with a sincerity of purpose which added to the poignancy of the fratricidal strife. But we are still very far from the goal to which Holism points. The great war, with its infinite loss and suffering, its toll of untold lives, the shattering of great States and almost of civilization, the fearful waste of goodwill and sincere human ideals which followed the close of that great tragedy—had been proof enough for our day and generation that we are yet far off the attainment of the ideal of a really Holistic universe. But, everywhere, too, I have seen that it was at bottom a struggle for the Good, a wild stirring towards human betterment; that blindly, and through blinding mists of passion and illusions, men are yet sincerely, earnestly, groping towards the light, towards the ideal of a better, more secure life for themselves and their fellows. Thus the League of Nations, the chief constructive outcome of the Great War, is but the expression of the deeply felt aspiration to a more stable holistic state of society. And the faith has been strengthened in me that what has here been called Holism is at work even in the conflicts and confusions of men; that in spite of all appearances to the contrary, eventual victory is serenely and securely waiting, and that the immeasurable sacrifices have not been in vain. The groaning and travailing of the Universe is never aimless or resultless. Its profound labours mean new creation, the slow painful birth of wholes, of new and higher wholes, and the slow but steady realisation of the Good which all the wholes of the Universe in their various grades dimly yearn and strive for.

"It is in the nature of the Universe to strive for and slowly, but in ever increasing measure, to attain wholeness, fullness, blessedness. The real defeat for men, as for other grades of the Universe would be to ease the pain by a cessation of effort, to cease from striving towards the Good. The holistic nisus which rises like a living fountain from the very depths of the Universe is the guarantee that failure does not await us, that the ideas of Well-being, of Truth, Beauty and Goodness are firmly grounded in the nature of things, and will not eventually be endangered or lost. Wholeness, healing, holiness—all expressions and ideas springing from the same root in language, as in experience—lie on the rugged, upward path of the Universe, and are secure of attaining it—in part here and now, and eventually more fully and truly. The rise and perfection of wholes in the Whole is the slow but unerring process and goal of this Holistic Universe."

Since this was written, even worse calamities have befallen us: but Smuts himself and those who share his noble belief in human progress have never faltered in the struggle for a better, kinder and more holistic world.

Chapter 9

Coalition with Hertzog: Heading for War

ALTHOUGH DURING his nine years out of office, Smuts found time, not only to complete his philosophical work on *Holism and Evolution*, but also by his lecturing tours in Great Britain and America to act as a missionary both of the Empire and of the League of Nations; yet he never neglected his duties as leader of the opposition in the South African parliament. He took part in the heated discussions on the Union Flag Bill which lasted through the three sessions of 1925–27, and, with Hertzog and Tielman Roos, finally settled the difficulty by the compromise flag, which, though hardly inspiring as a national emblem, at any rate allayed the respective susceptibilities of the Dutch- and British-born citizens and averted a threatened secession from the Union by Natal.

On the far more important question of the natives' rights, and especially their exercise of the franchise, on which Hertzog introduced four bills in 1926, Smuts was critical not so much of Hertzog's principles as of his methods of dealing with the difficulties: but at any rate Smuts's criticisms of Hertzog's proposals and the still more fundamental objections of the ardent defenders of the natives' rights, such as Rose Innes, formerly chief justice at the Cape, and Hofmeyr, one of Smuts's own most faithful supporters in other respects, caused the postponement of a final decision on Hertzog's proposals for another ten years, by which time Hertzog, Smuts and Hofmeyr were colleagues in the same ministry.

Meanwhile Hertzog seemed more firmly established in power than ever by his success in the general election of 1929; a result at which Smuts was frankly disappointed. But he agreed with Hertzog in deploring Great Britain's refusal at the Imperial Conference of 1930, to consider a policy of colonial preference, and went so far as to say that "What might have been the most brilliant, the most successful and greatest of all Imperial Conferences has ended in disillusion and disappointment for every part of the British Commonwealth . . . If the final settlement of Dominion status had gone hand in hand with a great gesture of fellowship and comradeship, with the holding out and the grasping of a helping hand all round in this common hour of trial, what a landmark the Conference would have been in the history of the Empire."[1] But at any rate he had the satisfaction of finding that Hertzog agreed with him in welcoming Balfour's definition of the Empire at the previous conference of 1926 as "autonomous communities within the British Empire, equal in status, in no way subordinate one to another in any aspect of their domestic or external affairs, though united by a common allegiance to the Crown and freely associated as members of the British Commonwealth of Nations," a definition finally given the force of law in the Statute of Westminster of 1931.

But by 1931 Hertzog's majority had begun to disintegrate. By that year the general slump in trade had spread to South Africa, and the Labour members who had hitherto supported him declared that their pact with him was at an end. Smuts was one of the first to realise that the maintenance of the gold standard, already abandoned by Great Britain, would lead the country into bankruptcy. But Hertzog obstinately clung to it and was supported by a report from a packed committee of parliament. Natal, disgusted with Hertzog's policy, again threatened secession, and even Hertzog's Nationalist party was getting restive; a by-election at Germiston, regarded as a safe Nationalist seat, was won by Smuts's South African party. Then appeared the man who regarded himself as the *Deus ex machina* to settle the country on a secure basis— Tielman Roos, a former minister under Hertzog, who had recently accepted a judgeship, which he now resigned with the intention of securing a coalition government from

[1] Quoted in *Annual Register*, 1930.

Hertzog's Nationalist and Smuts's South African party, under his own leadership.

Smuts himself also called on Hertzog to resign and to make a new start with a really national government on non-racial lines, for, as he told the House in February, 1933, South Africa's economic plight was so parlous that it could be cured only on national lines by a merger of his own South African party with Hertzog's Nationalists: "if there is a general election," he said, "I do not fear the result; but even with a complete victory for my party, people will feel that bitterness will remain. There is no way towards a change except through the resignation of the government"; and that then, not Roos, nor himself should be prime minister, but that Hertzog should resume office as head of a coalition government taken from Hertzog's and his own parties. Accordingly, at this time, as always, great as the temptation may have been, he carefully abstained from saying anything bitter about his opponents, as he might have had good excuse for doing: for he always remained faithful to the great aim that he and Botha had set before themselves, to have a real union between the two European races in South Africa.

And so it was arranged in that same year, 1933, no more being heard of Roos, who was then almost a dying man. But then came a hitch. Hertzog naturally offered high office in the new cabinet to his old rival Smuts, as leader of the South African party: but Smuts himself, who had been in opposition to Hertzog for more than twenty years was at first unwilling to serve under him and even thought of retiring from politics altogether, in spite of his party's urgent demand that he should still lead them. Finally, however, after a climb on his beloved Table Mountain with a couple of old and trusted friends to think things out in peace, he decided that, if there were no other reason, he could not leave in the lurch such faithful supporters as Patrick Duncan, Hofmeyr and Deneys Reitz, who had decided, on his own advice, to join the new ministry. So he accepted Hertzog's offer that he should take the post of deputy prime minister. Smuts himself said of his own party, which, in the general election of 1933, obtained a majority, "we deliberately gave up certain victory for the sake of peace and co-operation between the two white races of South Africa."[2]

For the next six years Smuts and Hertzog worked together in the same ministry. Hertzog by this time seemed to have become quite reconciled to the inclusion of South Africa within the British Empire on the lines laid down by Balfour in 1926; he had come to recognise that for the financial stability of the Union the abandonment of the gold standard, as Smuts had urged, was essential. On the great question of the abolition of the parliamentary franchise for natives, which had been hanging fire for nearly ten years, and the substitution of some more effective means of securing the representation of native views and interests, there appeared to be no fundamental divergence between them, though, in fact, Smuts is more liberal-minded on native questions than Hertzog; but he agreed to Hertzog's native policy for fear of breaking up the ministry. Undoubtedly, during these six years, Smuts though occupying only the second place in the ministry, was the master-mind of the cabinet: as Hertzog himself said to J. W. Lamont, an American writer well acquainted with South African conditions: "Yes, I have the title [of prime minister], but it is General Smuts who runs the Government."[3] In private Hertzog could be a pleasant companion—he was well-read and, like Smuts, had, as we have seen, more than a bowing acquaintance with the classics; but in politics he was of an uneasy and somewhat jealous temperament and apt to resent criticism by his colleagues. As Reitz said of him: "He was a man of culture and a gentleman, but of an uneasy temperament, and there were frequent crises when some of our colleagues resigned; he never realised that his wing of the Unity party was a minority kept in power."[4] Smuts, on the other hand, throughout the six years of the coalition showed real statesmanship in the vital effort on which he

[2] D. Reitz, *op. cit.*, 167–70 (on election).

[3] Quoted by J. W. Lamont in *Saturday Review of Literature*, N.Y., 6 May, 1944.

[4] D. Reitz, 230 ff.

was engaged to get Dutch and English to work together, and was determined not to break up the coalition except on a question of national importance.

In this coalition government's first six years, when the country was at peace externally and internally, important schemes for developing home industries and natural resources were carried out with great success. The Vaal-Harts irrigation scheme, originally projected by Rhodes, was carried to completion chiefly under Reitz's supervision, whereby, at a cost of £6,000,000, a vast inland sea of some ninety miles of fresh water was created to irrigate a specially thirsty land. Reitz too was largely responsible for developing the great Kruger National Park, where visitors in their motor-cars can drive in perfect safety to within a stone's throw of lions, buffaloes, giraffes, hippopotami and every kind of deer, though they are ranging where they list in perfect liberty. Sometimes Reitz would persuade Smuts to accompany him on an aeroplane jaunt of inspection, when the two friends chaffed each other, enjoying themselves like a couple of schoolboys. The only pastime in which Reitz would not join his chief was mountaineering, and he had the laugh of him once when he found him in bed with two doctors attending him for overstrain on Table Mountain, and quoted to him the Japanese saying: "He who hasn't climbed Fujiyama once is a fool, and he who climbs him twice is a damned fool."[5]

In 1935 Hertzog introduced the government's two measures for dealing with the native question: (1) the Natives' Representation Bill, and (2) the Native Trust and Land Bill. By the first Bill it was proposed to abolish the franchise hitherto allowed to educated natives in the Cape and Natal, except in the case of individual natives then living and already exercising it. In Natal, it is true, the native franchise had always been a farce, applying to only a handful of natives; but in the Cape it actually gave the natives entitled to the vote a majority in certain constituencies; though in fact, as the representatives they

[5] *Ibid.*, 196–210.

elected were exclusively of European origin, these representatives, after election, rarely paid much attention to their native constituents' interests. It was proposed, however, as compensation for the loss of voting power, to set up a Natives' Representative Council, empowered not only to discuss native needs and grievances for representation to the government but also to elect four European senators to represent their views in the South African parliament. This Bill aroused a good deal of opposition, not only among the educated natives of the Cape, but also from an important section of the white community, especially in the Cape Province, which for long had prided itself on having enfranchised educated natives. The opposing partisans were led by the veteran ex-chief justice, Sir James Rose Innes, and supported by Smuts's friend J. H. Hofmeyr, who resigned from the ministry on this question. Smuts, speaking on this Bill, emphasised the important rôle of the proposed Natives' Representative Council, as providing for the first time a platform for the expression of genuine native opinion and wants. The second, Native Trust and Land, Bill was intended to create a trust for securing more land for native settlements. Such a measure was urgently needed since, according to the official statistics of 1929, while the European population of the Union was 22.4 per cent. of the total population, that of the natives amounted to 67.9 per cent., whereas the land available for native settlement was at best in inverse proportion. By this Native Trust and Land Bill more land was to be gradually acquired to remedy this glaring discrepancy: but, though the Bill was passed, it does not appear that the natives have yet acquired a sensible, or at any rate a sufficient, increase of land.

In some respects the Natives' Representation Act has been of advantage to the natives. Smuts himself went to preside at the first meeting of their Representative Council in December, 1937, and for the first time the native community was able to feel that serious attention was being paid to their needs and grievances. Moreover, there is no doubt that in parliament itself the presence of representatives elected by the Native Council, such as Mrs. Ballinger

—who for years has been devoting her noble energies to improving the lot of the natives in compounds at Johannesburg and other cities where there is a large demand for native workmen and servants, and generally looking after their interests—is attracting more serious attention to the needs of South Africa's largest, but, as far as rights go, most neglected population. It must be all the more galling to natives educated up to European standards at such colleges as that at Fort Hare, or of the calibre of the late Tengo Jabavu, that eminent native journalist, and of his son, Professor Davidson Jabavu, on the staff of the Hare University College or of native doctors who are sometimes consulted by European patients, to have been deprived of the Cape franchise. Smuts himself, as will appear later, has gradually, owing to his experience in the present war, begun to realise that a section, at any rate, of this population deserves better treatment than has hitherto been allotted to it.

Meanwhile Germany was fast moving towards war, which Smuts, among the very few in South Africa, was beginning to realise might be inevitable. Hertzog, in his New Year message of 1937, took a highly optimistic view of the prospects of peace; Smuts was less hopeful. "Faith," he said, "in international co-operation and in collective security seems almost to have perished from the earth, and, in despair, the nations are rushing to arms and arming for safety."[6] Of one thing, however, Smuts was convinced, that if it came to war between Great Britain and Germany, South Africa must take her part on Britain's side, and in the general election of 1938 he made his position on that point perfectly clear. The aim of the government, he said, was to maintain the best relations with Great Britain and the British Commonwealth of Nations: "That position," he added, "is final. We are not thinking of secession. Even though some of our old republicans sometimes talk of republicanism, they have bound themselves in honour as members of our party and ad-

---

[6] *Annual Register*, 1937.

herents to our policy to stand by the British Commonwealth of Nations."

But as the prospect of war became clearer in 1939, a cleavage of view in the cabinet itself became apparent. In April, Hertzog made a speech indicating that, though the Union would never break with her greatest friend, Great Britain, she would not necessarily, in case of war, take up arms on Britain's side; Smuts, speaking at his birthplace, Malmesbury, a little later, declared emphatically that in such a case South Africa should and would fight with the mother-country. Then came the declaration of war by Great Britain against Germany on 3rd September, 1939.

At this juncture it was fortunate for Great Britain and for South Africa that the lawyers discovered that the life of the Senate would expire within a few weeks, and that, unless parliament met on 2nd September to extend its period of office, no legislation could be passed. It was fortunate because it appears to have been the intention of Hertzog, as head of the government, to declare, without consulting parliament or apparently even the cabinet, that, subject to certain contractual obligations to Great Britain, South Africa would remain neutral. Questioned by members on his policy at the first meeting of parliament on the 2nd, Hertzog postponed his answer in parliament for two days and summoned the cabinet for the 3rd September to hear his decision. According to Reitz, who gives a graphic account of the cabinet meetings,[7] Hertzog opened the discussion in the cabinet with a speech lasting three hours, in which he raked up all his grievances against England and praised Hitler's policy, and thereupon adjourned the discussion to the following day, when he again delivered a lengthy harangue on the policy he had chosen. Smuts, supported by Reitz, thereupon declared that he would test this decision in a parliamentary debate. When the House met, on 5th September, Hertzog, as he had informed the cabinet, moved that South Africa should remain neutral in the European war. He was followed by Smuts, then Deputy Prime Minister and Minister of Justice, who

[7] *No Outspan*, 230–44.

moved as an amendment: (1) that the Union's relations with Germany should be severed, (2) that the Union should carry out the obligations to which it had agreed and continue co-operation with the British Commonwealth of Nations, (3) that the Union should take all defence measures necessary, but not send forces overseas; and (4) that the Union's freedom and independence was at stake and that it should oppose force as an instrument of policy. After Reitz had supported Smuts's amendment a long debate ensued, and finally Smuts's motion was carried by eighty votes to sixty-seven. Thereupon Hertzog asked the Governor-General, Sir Patrick Duncan, to dissolve parliament and have a general election, a proposal rejected by Duncan owing to the critical state of affairs. Hertzog then had no alternative but to resign, and Smuts formed a new ministry, with himself as Prime Minister and Minister both of Defence and External affairs, and including his friend Reitz as Minister of Native Affairs and Hofmeyr of Finance and Education, while Colonel Stallard, of the Dominion Party, accepted the Ministry of Mines: it was a strong and united ministry which since then has lasted with very little change.

Nevertheless for the first year and a half of its existence Hertzog and his friends made no less than three more attempts to draw out of the war. In January, 1940, Hertzog moved "that the time had come for the war against Germany to be ended and for peace to be restored." Smuts in his reply emphasized that "no outside pressure of any kind [as Hertzog had suggested] had been put upon us . . . Great Britain had asked us for nothing, had given us no advice . . . but left the matter entirely to the free decision of the people of South Africa and so we have decided . . . The decision . . . is first and foremost in the interests of South Africa . . ." Germany was still anxious to recover her old colonies, especially South-West Africa, and "we have no hope of defending South-West Africa if Great Britain stands aside and if the British fleet is not helping us." Again, in August, 1940, after Dunkirk, Hertzog once more moved that South Africa should forthwith make peace with Germany and Italy, arguing that England was then without allies and had but the slenderest chance of victory against the powerful combination against her, while South Africa was "doomed like a second Sancho Panza to serve as Europe's imperial satellite on behalf of Europe's warmonger [England]." Smuts made a slashing reply, reprobating Hertzog for glorifying Germany, for "praising Herr Hitler to the skies," for proposing to take the "Petain road," and he reminded the House of German ambitions in Kenya, South-West Africa and of other dangerous designs in their continent. Hertzog's motion was this time defeated by eighty-three to sixty-five. One more attempt, the fourth and the most long-drawn of all, was made by Hertzog's friend, Dr. Malan, by a motion of no confidence in the government, the debate on which lasted from 4th to 7th February, 1941. Once more Smuts dwelt on the danger of German and, by this time, Italian ambitions in Africa, and, as a counterpoise, on the Union's increasingly good relations with the Portuguese and Belgian colonies, and above all on the closer relations between the British Commonwealth of Nations and the Americas, all to the advantage of their own country, for by sticking to Great Britain, he argued, South Africa would be able to develop as a young country without any compulsion. This time he defeated his opponents by seventy-six to fifty-eight.

In this last debate Hertzog took no part, for he was no longer in parliament. The leaders of the opposition, Pirow and Malan, who succeeded him, were even more ferocious opponents of the British connexion than himself. A week before this last debate Smuts had made a generous gesture to Hertzog, his former colleague and old opponent, in proposing that a pension should be voted to him in his retirement. He had not, he said, proposed it when Hertzog left the ministry in 1939, as it might have looked like a bribe. But now he felt free to eulogize Hertzog's clean fighting, unselfishness and public spirit: "our political and public life in South Africa in general is clean, clean of corruption," he said, echoing a somewhat similar eulogy by Rhodes of the Cape Parliament, as contrasted with "the methods of Australian and other colonies, where members indulge in vulgar personalities."[8] "We are pleased," concluded Smuts, "to do honour to General Hertzog as one of the most outstanding leaders the people of South Africa have ever had." Hertzog died less than two years later, in November, 1943.

[8] Quoted in my *Cecil Rhodes,* 188. The extracts from the speeches made in these debates are quoted from *House of Assembly Debates.*

Chapter 10

Smuts and the War in Africa

"EUROPE HAS landed itself in a terrible mess"; said Hertzog in May, 1940, "through the stupidity of General Smuts we are in it too." Smut's reaction was different: "Yes, I'm well, I'm ready. The time is here, and I'm ready . . . I am going to fight Germany; and I don't care where it is, so long as it is against Germany. Some want to fight it behind this river or behind that mountain, and hope to heaven the enemy is not there. But we want to fight Germany. She is the enemy and the enemy of the human race; Germany is our enemy and Africa is a big place in which to fight." Like Churchill, he had no doubt about the event. "The Germans will take Paris," he realized in May, 1940, "the Italians are in: we'll win the war." From the very beginning he was convinced first, that the U.S.A. were bound sooner or later, to come in and secondly that "you cannot defeat the English, because their hearts are too strong." Still he realised that in those early days it was a matter of touch and go, and quoted to a friend the prayer of Adam Kok, King of the Griquas: "God! in spite of all our prayers, we keep on losing our battles. Tomorrow we are fighting a really big battle. We need help very badly, God, and there is something I must say to You. Tomorrow's battle will be a serious affair. It will be no place for children. I ask You therefore not to send Your Son to help us. Come Yourself."

Unlike Churchill, he had no united country behind him. In June, 1940, when Germany was winning all along the line, "the Nazi opposition (in South Africa) have issued an appeal for surrender" it was recorded, "they propose to hold protest meetings and generally hinder the Government's war efforts. General Smuts," they say, "offers up South Africa once again—and perhaps for the last time— on the altar of imperialism, his personal lust for honour and his cold-blooded contempt for our country's most sacred interests. He now declares that he is prepared to make South Africa a partner in England's fate to the bitter end. The time has come to call a halt to General Smuts's mad progress."[1]

Smuts indeed was faced with a hard task when he undertook to bring his country into the war on the side of Great Britain. It is true that in each of the debates on the issue of a peace or war, recorded in the last chapter, he had carried the day by slightly increasing majorities, but in each of these debates it appeared that considerably more than a third of the members were, if not pro-German, at any rate violently opposed to any intervention on behalf of the Allies. But these figures hardly represented the real views of the country. According to an estimate made by Deneys Reitz[2] and subsequently verified by the election of 1943, of the total white population, consisting only of between two and three millions, fifty-five per cent. were of Dutch and forty-five per cent. of British descent; but of the fifty-five per cent. Dutch only about half stood aloof from the war effort, holding that the war was only in the interest of Great Britain and that there was no need for South Africa to be drawn into the mælstrom; the remaining half of the Dutch made common cause with the British population: in other words, about seventy-two per cent. of the white population were on Smuts's side for active participation in the war: but to the end the dissentient minority of twenty-eight per cent. was a heavy burden for Smuts to carry.

For one thing, though foiled in successive attempts to reverse the war policy, the extreme members of the opposition both in parliament and in the country, started more or less secret organisations with the avowed object of sabotaging the war effort. The most dangerous of these organisations was the so-called Ossewa-Brandwag (the

[1] The quotations in these two paragraphs are taken from Mrs. Millin's *World Black-out*, 1944, in which she records, in diary form, opinions she heard in South Africa during the first three years of the war.
[2] *No Outspan*, 276.

ox-wagon picket). This was started in 1938 by van Rensburg, then administrator of the Free State, for the comparatively innocuous purpose of celebrating the centenary of the Boers' great trek up country in 1838 to escape from British rule in Cape Colony. Smuts himself took part in this Boer national celebration, addressing, with van Rensburg, a great Boer gathering at Pietersburg on that occasion, and, it is related, after his speech joining his fellow-Boers at a huge bonfire where they all toasted sausages and sang patriotic songs: but, needless to say, he had no sympathy with the subsequent activities of Ossewa-Brandwag. For after 1939 it was used, not so much by van Rensburg himself, as by its extremist members, as an instrument for opposing Smuts's war policy, and for a time was active in sabotaging railways and factories, and even in beating up or murdering supporters of the government; in the early stages of the war it claimed to have as many as 250,000 members, and was obviously dangerous. It identified itself, as far as possible, with Hitler's Nazi organisation; its members adopted the Swastika badge, gave the Hitler salute, armed and drilled in secret, took up the slogan "Wir fahren nach England," threatened death to the Jews and the bureaucrats, had camps with barracks, each holding sixteen members of the organisation. "In fact," as Smuts said, "we are fighting this war not only at the front, but internally as well."[3] Some of the worst offenders, caught red-handed, suffered the due penalties of the law: but Smuts, supported by his friend Reitz, wisely thought it would be a mistake to take too drastic measures with the organisation as such, believing, as he said, the South Africans were too level-headed to be led astray by such nonsense, and that it would be a mistake to create cheap martyrs. "Leave it to us," he said, to those who urged the total suppression of the organisation, "Leave it to us, we know what we are doing: please don't rock the boat."[4]

In one respect, however, the Germans played into

[3] Millin, *The Reeling Earth*, 66-7.
[4] D. Reitz, *op. cit.*, 256 ff.

Smuts's hands. They had not forgotten that their two colonies of German South-West and German East Africa had been lost in the previous war, and made no secret of their intention to recapture them and so once more to become a menace to South Africa itself; and few even of the most rabid anti-British Boers were keen to have such uneasy neighbours once more on their borders. Already too, the German Navy and its swarms of U-boats were threatening South African communications with Europe and the East, which the British Navy, then barely holding its own in the Atlantic and the Mediterranean, was in no position to safeguard. The loss, in October, 1940, of Dakar, the most westerly French port on the Atlantic, "as important in its way as Suez," as Smuts said, "involved all our movements in the Atlantic."[5] All these dangers were clear enough to him, who, at the outset and throughout the war, tried to bring home to his people that, if for no other reason, it was essential for their own safety and practical independence, within or outside the British Empire, to resist German and Italian aggression. Smuts no doubt himself realized from the earliest days of the war, that it could not be confined to separate compartments of the globe, and that a defeat of the Germans and Italians in Europe would bring their designs on other parts of the world to nought even more effectively than victories in Africa. But he had to work with the tools available at any given moment, and realized that, with his people divided his most effective appeal to them for the time being was to bring home to them their own peculiar danger from the Axis powers on the continent of Africa. And so at first it was agreed on Smut's own motion in parliament that, while South African soldiers might be called upon to fight anywhere in Africa, they should not be sent outside their own continent.

Not content with calling on his own people to defend their heritage, he realized that German ambitions might very well affect other parts of South Africa. As early as

[5] *Ibid.,* 29, 30.

1924 he had, as we have seen, tried to induce Southern Rhodesia to join in a common policy with the Union on matters of defence, etc., but had then found no response.[6] Now, however, with the threat from common enemies to all British possessions in Africa, he found a readier response. "Now is the time," said Smuts, "for us to readjust our outlook on African affairs and to develop a new conception of our relations with our neighbours . . . We cannot stand aloof, we of this richly-endowed South Africa. If we wish to take our rightful place as leader in Pan-African development and in shaping future policies and events in this vast continent, we must face realities of the present and seize the opportunities which those offer."[7] This time his proposal was welcomed. In a gesture of complete trust the South Rhodesian government confided their armed forces to the command of General Smuts; and Sir Godfrey Huggins, their prime minister, worked in close co-operation with Smuts and his ministers. Similar co-operation was agreed upon between South Africa and the crown colony of Northern Rhodesia, with Nyasaland and even the distant Kenya, where South African troops were lining the borders against Abyssinia even before the Italian threat had materialised. Smuts also extended his invitations to co-operation in the defence of African interest against German and Italian ambitions to the Belgian Congo and the Portuguese provinces of Angola and Lourenço Marques, invitations which were glady accepted. So effective had this new policy of co-operation among all the anti-Nazi communities throughout the African continent become that in September, 1943, Smuts was able to present it as an accomplished fact. "The most striking thing about Africa to-day," he said, "is the new conception which is slowly growing up. People are no longer thinking in terms of sovereignties and flags, but of common action and common interest. . . . In Africa, to-day, South Africa, the Rhodesias, the Congo and the Portu-

[6] See above, Chapter 8.

[7] *Annual Register,* 1940.

guese colonies are gradually evolving common policies on matters such as trade, transport, communications and native affairs. This means a complete reversal of the old Roman theory, whereby you had Imperium or sovereignty first, and then ruled the country as you wanted it. Now the countries work together in harmony on common principles, without seeking to conquer each other or upset local loyalties, or languages, or methods of administration."[8]

There was indeed much leeway to be made up in providing even for the defence of South Africa itself. As early as 1924 an agreement had been made by Smuts and Churchill that instead of the British admiralty South Africa should thenceforward be responsible for the defence of the naval base at Simonstown: but it was not till the outbreak of war in 1939, that the Union created a Seaward Defence Force for patrolling the coast, minesweeping, etc., a force which soon proved very effective against German and, later, Italian sea-marauders. An even more important change was made in the duties of the South African defence force. As this force was originally constituted by Smuts himself in 1912, it was doubtful whether it could be required to act outside the borders of South Africa;[9] accordingly he now started a new army on a voluntary system, whereby recruits undertook to serve "anywhere in Africa," so as to be available to resist any encroachments by the Italians from Abyssinia or the Germans from overseas on British or Allied possessions in Africa. This re-organisation proved an immense success: recruits of both Dutch and English lineage flocked to the colours; and every man or woman embodied in this new African defence force wore the "orange flash," indicating willingness to serve anywhere in the African continent. In fact, by March, 1944, Smuts was able to claim in the South African Parliament that one out of every three

[8] Quoted from *South Africa*. A more detailed exposition of Smuts's view in this respect was given by Mr. Heaton Nichols at Chatham House on *The Part of the Union in the Development of Africa*, on 27 March, 1945.

[9] See above, Chapter 5.

South Africans between twenty and sixty had volunteered for the forces; "an incredible feat," as he called it.

An important subsidiary to this force was obtained by the voluntary enrolment of natives, unarmed, indeed, but of the greatest service for work as pioneers, and signalmen and for road-making and transport. Among the tribes most forward in supplying men for these pioneer corps were Swazis and Basutos, and besides them there were Indians domiciled in South Africa; and all were proud of the valiant help they were able to give. As a Basuto Sergeant in a Pioneer Signals Company said: "We belong to the Eighth Army. We charged their batteries, drove their trucks, unloaded their signal stores, carried their telegraph poles, mended their wires. We were bombed with them, we enjoyed the same rations, we laughed at the same jokes, we were blown up by the same mines."[10] By January, 1943, no less than 70,000 African tribesmen were serving in the army and of "coloured" troops (i.e., Indians or Malays), as many as 45,000.

Apart from the voluntary forces enlisted for the defence of Africa, of which South Africans are justly proud, they have also cause for pride in the readiness with which, under the inspiration of their great ruler, they turned a country hitherto chiefly concerned with internal and mainly peaceful interests into a veritable arsenal for total warfare. The rapid development of the seaward defence forces and of a new army prepared to fight anywhere in Africa has already been noted: but these activities form only a small part of South Africa's contribution to victory. Smuts himself has always been air-minded, and, as we have seen,[11] has some right to be called the father of the Royal Air Force of Great Britain. During the twenty years interval of peace he delighted in long air-borne voyages in South Africa, often with his dear friend Deneys Reitz: nevertheless at the outbreak of the second war in 1939, the supply of operational craft and trained pilots in South

[10] Quoted from *South Africa* of 4 Sept. 1943.
[11] See above. Chapter 7.

Africa was alarmingly short. Accordingly he at once set about repairing deficiencies, aiming first at three complete squadrons, partly for patrolling thousands of miles of coast-line and safeguarding the all-important Cape route by sea, partly for active operations on land. So effective were these measures that within twenty-four hours of the outbreak of war with Italy, South African airmen were raiding Italian bases in Abyssinia and Somaliland, and, though greatly outnumbered by the Italian air force, almost from the outset established complete air superiority. By August, 1941, on the South African Air Force's twenty-first birthday, Smuts could claim that it contained 27,000 personnel and would eventually number some 50,000—a remarkable contribution from a population of some 2,250,000.

In many other respects South Africa made valuable contributions to the war effort. Already, during Hertzog's last ministry, the great Iron and Steel Corporation, *Iscor*, near Pretoria, was starting an important new industry, so was fully prepared to switch off to manufacturing armour-plate, steel helmets, shells and spare parts of equipment, besides providing most of the steel required for factories engaged in producing howitzers, mortars, armoured cars, etc. Hence, South Africa was soon prepared, not only to supply most of its own military requirements, but also through the British government or the Eastern Supply Council to bring help to other fronts. In fact, by 1942 South Africa had become the repair shop for the Middle East.[12] The manufacture of explosives, needed in great quantities by the mines in peace time, was easily switched off to provide some of the vast quantities of ammunition required in such a war. With the restrictions now inevitable on importation from other countries, new industries had to be improvised to supply necessities. Paper for example, for which South Africa depended largely on Norway, suddenly became alarmingly scarce; accordingly three new factories, equipped with special machinery,

[12] *Annual Register,* 1942.

were established, one of which was soon able to provide some 12,000—14,000 tons of paper and cardboard annually. South Africa, the home of diamonds, used to export to Holland, the headquarters of the world's diamond-cutters, most of the diamonds needed for industrial purposes, such as lens-cutting and various processes in munition factories; but with the capture of Holland by the Germans, this outlet was closed; accordingly, in May, 1942, a factory was established in Johannesburg for this special industry. The most curious of all these new industries was that on which three men of the South African Medical Corps were employed in catching and extracting serum from cobras, puff-adders and mambas, the most dangerous snakes in South Africa, for the manufacture of the very necessary anti-snakebite serum for men bitten in many of the snake-haunted districts of Africa.

The work, too, of the women of South Africa, as in other countries, has been an indispensable adjunct of the war effort. In November, 1939, the Women's Auxiliary Army Service and the Women's Auxiliary Air Force, each with a membership soon amounting to 5,000 were officially constituted. The ease and rapidity with which these services were organised were, however, due to the foresight of South African women more than a year earlier. Already in 1938 they realised that war was impending, and immediately began, as the South African Women's Auxiliary Service, registering the names of women willing, in case of need, to give their help. Thus, when war was actually declared, the government was presented with a comprehensive register of women volunteers, with thousands of names card-indexed into categories of service, thereby enormously assisting the rapid organisation of the two women's corps for service with the army and the air force and of those required for munitions work, or as operators of delicate technical instruments in the coastal defence system, quite apart from the many women engaged in the new factories and industries needed for the war effort.

The Union indeed might well be proud of its contributions to the war effort of the Allies. In June, 1943, it was officially stated that the Union defence force had a total strength of 169,000 European men and women—not including 30,000 discharged—50,000 volunteers on part-time service, and 60,000 in the women's auxiliary services. With only 570,000 males between twenty and sixty years of age the number of 190,000 males volunteering for service (one in three of the age group) was unsurpassed by any of the Allied Nations. Of these 86,000 had served in East Africa, the Middle East and Madagascar. In addition, 30,000 of the 102,000 volunteers from the Malay, Indian and native communities had served outside South Africa. War supplies valued at £100,000,000 had been sent to Britain and the Allies, including armoured cars supplied to British and French units in Africa and in Burma. In addition, there were 130 factories of army clothing and equipment, and mass production of foodstuffs for home and abroad.[13]

Over all these new activities, as well as over the military activities of the Union in Africa itself and beyond, brooded the spirit of South Africa's great prime minister; and his tireless exertions were well supported by the united cabinet he had created. It is no derogation to the value of the other members to pick out two of them as those on whom he specially relied, Hofmeyr and Deneys Reitz. Hofmeyr had, as noted above, withdrawn for a time from the coalition cabinet under Hertzog, feeling as he did so strongly on the native question, as well as on a somewhat dubious appointment to the cabinet: but when Smuts had formed his cabinet he soon returned to office and eventually, as Minister of Finance, proved singularly effective in providing funds for his chief's warlike efforts. Deneys Reitz, Smuts's dearest friend, became deputy prime minister, and also took over the portfolio of native affairs; but when, in 1942, there was a vacancy in the office of High Commissioner in London, Smuts chose him for this part. No choice could have been happier, for though Reitz had

[13] These figures are taken from the *Annual Register*, 1943.

at first, after Vereeniging, remained a *bitter-ender* and taken up a job as transport rider in Madagascar, he had, after being nursed through a dangerous illness for a year by Smuts and his wife, become entirely converted to his host's broader and wiser outlook. In fact, during the last war he had taken part in Smuts's campaign in German South Africa and eventually became colonel of a Guards battalion on the western front. As High Commissioner in London, he was an ideal representative of his country, courteous and accessible to all, and, while jealously guarding the independent rights of his dominion, doing more than any previous High Commissioner, except perhaps Schreiner, in strengthening the bonds of union between Great Britain and South Africa. His sudden death in October, 1944, was a grievous loss to both countries. To Smuts himself, to whom he was the dearest of companions, probably the only one in these strenuous days intimate enough to relieve something of the stress of war by his genial, boyish chaff and deep affection, this sudden death came very hard. In a tribute to him Smuts spoke of him as "a dear friend and comrade, a faithful companion through vicissitudes such as few have passed through. He was true, straight and upright—every inch of him—and he leaves a personal memory which I shall cherish all my days." To us in England, he is best known by his three delightful tales of adventure and good companionship, *On Commando, Trekking On* and *No Outspan*, which rank with Sir Percy Fitzpatrick's *Jock of the Bushveld* as the most engaging pictures we have of South African scenery and personalities at their best.[14]

South Africans were justly proud of their men's achievements in the war against Germans and Italians in their own continent. When Italy entered the war South African forces were ready for them on the borders of Kenya and took their part in driving the Italians out of their ill-gotten

[14] The concluding words of this paragraph were written immediately after the touching memorial service to Deneys Reitz at St. Martin-in-the-Fields, a service partly in Dutch, partly in English, on 25 October, 1944.

possession of Abyssinia. In switching off to Northern Africa they still had to deal with Italians in Tripoli, but were also ranged against the far more formidable Germans under Rommel. In May, 1942, two South African brigades were captured in Tobruk, whereupon Smuts in a broadcast appealed—not vainly—for 7,000 recruits to come forward to fill the gaps; in September Tobruk was recaptured and the 1st South African Division under General Pienaar had the honour of being the first to re-enter the town. Already in June the South African Brigade of the 8th Army had borne the brunt of the successful fight at Alamein, but in Montgomery's final victory at the same place the South African forces were too depleted to share in the victory. When, however, after this defeat, Rommel was in full retreat from North Africa, there was nothing left for Smuts's reorganised army, with its "orange flash," to do on their own continent except tedious garrison work. But by that time, as Smuts had foreseen, South Africans generally had awoken to the fact that such a war, against such an enemy could not be confined to one continent. They were proud of their army and proud of its commander-in-chief, as was shown in 1943 by a gift of £250,000 raised from voluntary subscriptions to Smuts personally, a gift which he handed over for the use of the troops.

Smuts himself had always realized that a victory for Hitler in Europe or for Japan in the Pacific might be just as fatal to South African security as a complete defeat in Africa. Accordingly in May, 1942, he had sanctioned the embarkation of a South African detachment on the fleet commanded by Admiral Syfret, himself a South African by birth, to secure the French province of Madagascar, dangerously close to South Africa, from falling into the hands of the Japanese. In January, 1943, he was attacked in Parliament for this apparent breach of the understanding that South Africans should not fight outside Africa,[15] but easily carried the House with him, when he pointed

[15] See above, p. 118.

out the imminent danger it would be to the country to have the Japanese within such easy reach of South Africa. Encouraged by this success, a fortnight later he moved that the general ban imposed on South African troops from fighting outside their own continent should be repealed so that they could carry on the pursuit of the Germans and Italians, then driven out of North Africa, into Sicily and Italy, reminding the House that Great Britain's Navy and Air Force were still contributing a large part to the security of the South Africans' own coastline: and that it was impossible to mark out a total war such as this into watertight compartments. After the debate, to which the opposition contributed most of the fifty-two speeches made, Smuts carried his motion by a handsome majority.

Accordingly, from 1943 onwards, South African troops were fighting as gallantly as ever in the Middle East, notably in the easy conquest of Sicily and the correspondingly arduous and bitterly-contested campaign in Italy. As Smuts declared, after one of his visits to the Italian front, "I have seen for myself something of the terrain over which our (6th) division has been advancing often through rain and mud over the mountains and deep valleys. They have accomplished prodigious feats. They have maintained their pursuit in country where every feature has favoured the defence . . . We can be justly proud of this crack division, rivalling in prowess our First and Second Divisions in North Africa." Throughout the war, indeed, Smuts himself always made a point of heartening the troops by visits to them in the forefront of operations, whether in Africa or in Europe.

Encouraged by his majority in the debate of January, 1943, Smuts decided to have a general election in the autumn of 1943 in spite even of Reitz's advice that the risk of reducing his majority was too great; to which he replied: "We are fighting for liberty and I am going on with it." This decision was more than justified by the event. In the old parliament he could reckon at most on eighty-four supporters against an opposition of sixty-six: by the new general election he increased his own United

Party to eighty-nine with general support from Labour, Dominion and Independent parties numbering eighteen more, while the opposition had dwindled to forty-three.[16]

Smuts owed this notable electoral success chiefly, no doubt, to the resounding success of his policy, partly also to his tactful dealing with the opposition in parliament and its intestine feuds. The three most prominent members of the opposition were Van Rensburg, the founder of Ossewa-Brandwag,[17] who had been Administrator of the Orange Free State province, Pirow and Malan, who had been ministers in Hertzog's cabinet. Van Rensburg himself was a man with a sense of responsibility and, though opposed to the war, on the whole acted on constitutional lines, though in the first two years of the war many of the members of his Ossewa-Brandwag were guilty of sabotage on the railways and even murder, being to some extent influenced by one Leibbrandt, an extremist and a noted boxer, said to have been landed from a German U-boat, but now locked up in gaol. Pirow was at first the most dangerous of Smuts's opponents, he had been an able minister and already before the war, when he visited Germany, had come under Hitler's influence: but now being no longer in parliament, with but a small personal following, he is much less formidable. Malan, a very eloquent and sincere man, the only one of the trio still in parliament, is endeavouring to gather together the various sections of the opposition to form a united party. Smuts himself, though respected, was perhaps still, as his best friend once told me in the early years of the war, hardly popular in his own country. He is, and always will be, too quick in sizing up the main points of policy to be pursued and in acting promptly on his decisions for his solid, slow-thinking Dutch fellow-countrymen; for he has never had the inspired patience of Botha in discussing with them at enormous length the pros and cons of policy. But his won-

---

[16] Later a by-election at Wakkerstroom, always an uncertain constituency, raised the opposition to forty-four.
[17] See above, p. 117.

derful success in the conduct of the war, his wisdom in allowing as much rope as possible to his opponents, a growing mellowness in his outlook, and above all, perhaps, his conviction of the major part to be played on the African continent by the Union are bringing even his opponents to recognize his patriotism and his wisdom. Though there are still, and no doubt will long remain, extremists in the two camps of British and Boer lineage, their number is gradually diminishing, owing partly to the great increase in mixed marriages, but chiefly to the increase of common interests in this war for self-preservation and to the wise tolerance of their great prime minister.

Chapter 11

Smuts on (1) Native and (2) Empire Problems; (3) Smuts at Home

(1) NATIVE PROBLEMS

TAKEN UP as he has been during the war with world affairs, Smuts, in spite of his seventy-five years, is still young enough in spirit to discover and attempt to remedy defects in the social and administrative conditions of his own beloved South Africa, especially in regard to the natives. It is, it may be admitted, hardly surprising that the South Africans of European lineage should have considerable uneasiness as to their security where the native population so greatly exceeds the Europeans. Smuts himself at one time shared these apprehensions, for it is related that, shortly after the Boer War, he and Botha, being much disturbed by rumours of a proposed native rising in the east, went to General Lyttelton, then G.O.C. in South Africa, to express their fears. "Don't you be worried," said the bluff old general, "we have managed somehow to beat you, so you need have no fear that we shall not be able to deal with a native rising." But Smuts himself soon shed his apprehensions, especially after many journeys into regions mostly inhabited by natives, which made him deeply interested in their customs. One of his daughters, when at college, visited the *Realm of the Rain Queen*, on which a Kriege nephew published a book in 1943, in a far-distant corner of East Africa, and he himself, stirred by their descriptions, visited this "wonderful woman," as he called her, "the rain-maker *par excellence* of South Africa, well over sixty, but strong in body and character, every inch a Queen." So enthusiastic was he that he wrote a preface to his nephew's book, finding it "a fascinating distraction to the war problems which form my life," and the Queen sent him a letter when he was prime minister, saying how glad she was to have met the man "wearing the crown of South Africa." Both he and Deneys Reitz in their travels and inspections before and during the war, sometimes together, sometimes separately, always made a point of getting into touch with the natives, especially in out-of-the-way districts, where they were at their simplest and best.

Lord Harlech, recently High Commissioner in charge of the three native territories, Basutoland, Swaziland and Bechuanaland, an acute and sympathetic observer of South African conditions, reckons the population of the Union itself at 10,000,000, of whom only two and a quarter millions are of European race—forty per cent. of these being English—and sixty per cent. Dutch-speaking—the remainder including 7,000,000 natives and some 500,000 so-called Cape coloured chiefly of mixed blood, including Malays and a small percentage of Hottentots, and some 250,000 Indians. Small as the proportion of Europeans is to other races in South Africa he points out that they are actually more in number than the total number of Europeans of all races throughout the whole of the rest of the continent, including even French North Africa. Unfortunately among these Europeans in South Africa is a considerable number of so-called "poor whites," who are mostly illiterate and have sunk below the level of many educated natives, but still cling to their rights as belonging to a *Herren Volk*. Considerable strides, as he points out, in providing education for the natives have recently been made; the great native college at Fort Hare in Cape Colony is a constituent of the University of South Africa and admits to full university degrees; and even in the Transvaal, which is not so advanced in outlook on native affairs as the Cape,[1] the Witwatersrand University has opened its medical faculty to the natives, especially in view of the great need of medical services in predominantly native districts.

The difficulties of race contact are most prominent where the natives are working in the mines or on the rail-

[1] Education, it must be remembered, is a provincial concern.

ways and other public works, and not least when serving as domestics in European households in the towns. In most of these services they are housed in compounds, often at a considerable distance from their work and not only destitute of any amenities, but overcrowded and sometimes barely in a sanitary condition. Something indeed has already been done to improve such conditions, largely through the devoted services of such workers as Mrs. Ballinger, who is one of the representatives of native interests in parliament: but there is still much leeway to make up. Those undertaking work on country farms are generally better off, living as they do on the farms, sometimes with their families, and on the whole carefully provided for by the farmers. Those living on the native reserves, such as the Transkei, where Rhodes's Glen Grey Act provided them with separate allotments and encouraged individual enterprise, are the best off in the Union. But so great is the demand for native labour, that a great many natives come in for periods of work from Zululand or from outside the Union, especially from Portuguese East Africa, and have for their term of service to live without their families.

One of the crying grievances of the natives domiciled within the Union, is the comparatively small amount of land reserved for them. When in 1936 the franchise was taken from them, as a partial compensation a Native Land Trust was established to hold 7,250,000 morgen (about 14,500,000 acres) of land for settlement by native families; but by 1943 only 3,000,000 morgen had been acquired for that purpose, most of it at a vast expense; for one farm, for example, in the Pietersberg district, valued at £89, the price was raised to £700 for the Land Trust and similar fantastic sums were demanded and paid in other districts.

Smuts himself, largely no doubt owing to the enthusiastic support by the native community of the war effort, and the gallantry of the unarmed native auxiliaries in the field, of which he had personally been witness in his visits to the front, made a striking confession in an address to the Institute of Race Relations at Cape Town in January, 1942.[2] Three views, he said, had hitherto been held in South Africa on the question of the policy to be adopted with natives: (1) for equality between the races, white and black; (2) for the theory of the superior race of the whites over the natives; (3) for trusteeship which Rhodes had proclaimed as the duty of whites as guardians of their black fellow-citizens who should be treated as wards; or, as was expressed in the Mandates Section of the League of Nations Covenant "the advancement, the upliftment of the backward peoples is the sacred trust of civilisation." This trusteeship was not merely, he added, an ethical or religious question, but one of self-interest for the trustee, who, if he neglected it, would sink to the level of his ward, and perpetuate the alienation between black and white. In two departments, he added, there was much leeway to make up—in education, though much had been done by the missionaries, the efforts of the government had been halting and tardy, while for health practically nothing had been done to prevent the heavy death rate of the native children and sickness of the adults, who, as he said, were "carrying the country on their backs"; and he called special attention to the need of improved health services and decent housing for natives in the urban districts and for more adequate wages and living conditions. "We have," he concluded, "accepted the idea of trusteeship; we must now begin to carry out our obligations"; and he found much encouragement for the future in "the excellent feeling in the armies of North Africa between natives, not only from South Africa," and their comrades of European descent.

Undoubtedly the growing claims of the natives for better conditions and more opportunity to control their own affairs are meeting a response from many of their Dutch and British fellow-citizens. Hofmeyr, one of Smuts's chief ministers, has always been the staunch apostle of native rights; of another minister and special confidant

---

[2] This speech has been published, and it is commented on in Alexander F. Campbell's *Smuts and the Swastika*, 1932.

of Smuts, Deneys Reitz, Minister of Native Affairs until he went to London as High Commissioner, the Native Representative Council recorded its "appreciation of the meritorious services [he] rendered to the cause of Bantu progress. By his courageous utterances on Union native policy and his obvious determination to see justice done to the African he did much to restore the confidence of the African people in the Ministry of Native Affairs." Then the presence in the South African Parliament of the earnest advocates elected as their representatives by the natives in council enables the native point of view to be effectively presented. In the Transvaal alone the number of native children in school has sensibly increased, and the Union grant for that purpose has risen by over £220,000 in three years. Enlightened mine managers, too, on the reef and other employers of native labour have for some years been improving the conditions of native labour and even encouraging the native workers to discuss their own wants and suggest improvements.[3]

In many other ways evidence is given, not only of the growing claims of the natives for better conditions of life and more opportunities to gain control of their own concerns, but also of the help given them to satisfy these claims by many of their Dutch and British South African fellow-citizens. *The South African Outlook,* "a monthly journal dealing with missionary and racial affairs," gives interesting particulars of native life, native grievances and more and more of the evident inclination not only of the government but also of some of the great industrial organisations to meet their just demands. We find in it, for example, an interesting report from a judicial commission on riots at the Pretoria municipal compounds, the main

[3] When I was on a visit to Johannesburg in 1936 I was privileged to attend a discussion group of native mine-workers on the Rand, in a club-room reserved for them by the managers, where there was no attempt to interfere with the free debate by any European. An address, on 28 February, 1945, by the High Commissioner for the Union of South Africa to the Royal Empire and Royal African Councils gives an encouraging account of recent advances in Native policy.

conclusions of which are that the city council should "improve the living conditions of its native employees," that the natives should have an "improved scale of rations," and that "an endeavour should be made to give reasonable satisfaction to the native demand for some voice in the management of their own affairs." It is encouraging, too, to read of a Johannesburg Joint Council of Africans and Europeans with its Bantu Children's Holiday Home at the seaside, where sick African children are sent for a couple of weeks' convalescence, of the raising of salaries for teachers in native secondary schools, of proposals for raising the very low pay of natives in the mines, and of no colour line being admitted for benefits by the South African Gifts and Comforts Fund and the South African Red Cross during the war. There is also a quarterly magazine, *Race Relations,* dealing with such subjects as the *Crisis in Native Education, Immigration and the Future of the Non-Europeans* and the *Record of a Joint Council* established in the mining district of Germiston "to promote the welfare of the country through discussion and co-operation between Europeans and non-Europeans." *E pur se muove.*

There is still of course a good deal of apprehension among many of the backveld and even of other South Africans who dread the danger of too well-educated natives rising in their millions against the much smaller dominant Anglo-Boer community, but the example set by Smuts, Hofmeyr and Deneys Reitz is gradually bringing home the almost certain truth that a general rise in native education and fairer dealing will only result in a more homogeneous community of South Africans, black as well as white, co-operating in an even more stable and self-respecting state.

(2) EMPIRE PROBLEMS

Smuts, like Churchill, has been an indefatigable traveller during the war, visiting his men wherever they might be fighting—in Africa or in Italy—heartening them by his presence and rejoicing in their successes. He also kept well in touch with the centre of the Empire by visits to England. His work indeed both for South Africa and for the British Commonwealth of Nations was fully recognised in May, 1941, by the award to him of the supreme military distinction of Field-Marshal in the British Army; though at home in South Africa he and his people still affectionately cling by preference to his title of General, the rank he held during the South African war as one of the outstanding leaders of a Boer commando, and also, after the Union, when he commanded British and Boer South African units in the East African campaign.

In his visits to England, as usual, he was called upon to address enthusiastic audiences, who were always heartened by his confident views on the ultimate results of the war and on the whole-hearted unity of the British Commonwealth of Nations. Among his speeches specially to be noted is his address to both Houses of Parliament on 21 October, 1942, in which he paid this notable tribute to our own Prime Minister and the spirit of our nation: "He [Churchill] remains the embodiment of the spirit of eternal youth and resilience, the spirit of a great undying nation in one of the greatest moments of history. Let us recognise with gratitude that we have been nobly blessed with wonderful leadership, both in the last war and in this . . . I speak of that inward glory, that splendour of the spirit which has shone over this land from the soul of its people . . . I feel I have come to a greater, prouder, more glorious home of the free than I ever learned to know in its palmiest days. This is the glory of the spirit, which sees and knows no defeat or loss but . . . sustains the will to final victory." In the concluding words of this speech he turns to the future of the world, expressing a hope that this struggle will bring about a new spirit of human solidarity between nations and result in much-needed improvements in our health, housing, education and decent social amenities: "May it be our privilege to see that this suffering, this travail and search of man's spirit shall not be in vain."

A year later, encouraged by the result of the general election in South Africa, he was able to spend some two months in England for further consultation on war plans. This time he was called upon to address a representative audience at the Guildhall in October, and to make another speech to a meeting of both Houses of Parliament in November. Now too he could speak with more assured confidence in a complete victory for the Allies and go on to consider the methods to adopt for securing the future peace of the world. Specially interesting and suggestive was the second of these addresses, in which he outlined his ideas about the future of the British Empire. Assuming that the end of the war would result in the predominance of the three great Powers, "Russia the colossus of Europe, Great Britain with her feet in all continents, but crippled materially here in Europe, and the United States of America with enormous assets, with wealth and resources and potentialities of power beyond measure," he is specially concerned with the future of Great Britain. In Europe he foresees that Great Britain, as contrasted with Russia and the United States with their vast internal resources, will be weak in her European resources, and suggests that we should strengthen ourselves here "by working closely together with the smaller democracies in Western Europe, which are of our way of thinking, . . . but which by themselves may be lost, as they are lost to-day, and as they may be lost again." In this way Great Britain, he believes, may still, as protector and close ally of these liberal democracies, preserve her position as one of the great pacific powers of Europe. Turning then to Great Britain's supreme source of strength as leader of the world-wide agglomeration of self-ruling states and dependencies within the British Empire, he has nothing but praise for "the strength of soul, the inner freedom" which characterize the free relations between the Mother Country and her self-governing Dominions. But, as he had said as early as 1930, "the last ten years have been devoted to the elaboration and perfection of the freedom of the Dominions; the next ten years should be given to the elaboration of co-operation within the Commonwealth."

On the other hand, as opposed to this principle of decentralization, there is the closely centralized system of our Colonial Empire, scattered as it is all over the globe; and he doubts whether such a dual system can endure within the Empire centralized and the Commonwealth decentralized. Accordingly he suggests that it is necessary to reduce the number of independent colonial units and group others, "and so tidy up the show." In this connection Smuts's abortive attempt in 1923 to induce the new self-governing colony of Southern Rhodesia to join up with the Union[4] will be remembered. Now he was in a much stronger position for pressing his suggestion for "tidying up the show." Southern Rhodesia had already gone so far as to put its war contingents under his command.[5] Since then the Colonial Office has recently established a consultative council to discuss the common interests of the Southern and Northern Rhodesias and Nyasaland; and Southern Rhodesia is already demanding that these three colonies should be amalgamated under one government.[6] If such an amalgamation took place it would no doubt be but the prelude to the design attributed to Smuts, though never so far expressed by him publicly, of comprehending within the Union of South Africa itself these three northern colonies, which, with the addition of South-West Africa, already mandated to the Union, would create a Dominion, or Union, for the whole of Southern Africa.

To Smuts himself and to South Africans generally no doubt the most pressing scheme for "tidying up the show" relates to the three native territories, Basutoland, Swaziland and Bechuanaland, which, though on or within the borders of the Union, are still under a High Commissioner sent from England. South Africa has long been anxious to incorporate them within the Union, a transfer which no doubt would long ago have been effected, were it not for the fact that all three tribes prefer to remain under the Imperial government. It remains to be seen how far the more liberal native policy urged by Smuts[7] will remove their objections, and satisfy Downing Street.

---

[4] See above, Chapter 8.
[5] See above, Chapter 10.
[6] An interesting leading article in *South Africa* of 28th October, 1941, presses for such a solution.
[7] See above, pp. 133.

Suggestive, too, was the *Letter* which, at the request of the Council for Education in World Citizenship, Smuts sent on Armistice Day, 1943, to *the Youth of Britain*. Recalling that twice before he had been invited to send similar letters—in 1931, "when the small storm cloud was gathering far away in Manchuria," in 1937, "when the threatening storm centre had passed to Africa, to Abyssinia; and now when the storm has burst and spread over the whole world . . . so do small mistakes lead in the end of their immeasurable consequences." Telling of a talk he had recently "with one of the greatest scientists in the world"[8] who had escaped from the Nazis, he found him "strangely optimistic; in spite of the catastrophe which had so suddenly overtaken them; they felt that England was bound to win in the end, and that all they had lost would be recovered again . . . Millions have lost their lives, many more millions have lost all hope, and drift along like dumb, driven cattle. But something remains, greater than disaster, greater than all the countless losses. It is faith, faith in our cause, faith in good, faith in God. Truly it is no world to-day for easy optimism, but for holding on with both hands and with our very souls to the things we believe in, the things which have raised us above the mere animal level, and have never let us down. Faith is the password"; a truly heartening message and one that no man more than Smuts is justified in handing down to the young.

Both as leader of his country and as far-seeing statesman of the Empire, Smuts was naturally called upon to play an important part in formulating the post-war settlement. Arriving in London on 3 April, 1945, in his aeroplane which, incidentally, had been struck by lightning in the middle of Africa, he attended an Empire conference before proceeding to the San Francisco Convention which was to draw up the Charter of the United Nations. There his main work was as president of the commission to deal with all matters connected with the General Assembly, which included provisions for security, the creation of a

[8] Einstein presumably.

Social and Economic Council and the system of Trusteeship. He was also in demand for consultation and discussion on the numberless difficult problems which cropped up in other departments of the Convention, and was entrusted with the drafting of the Charter's Preamble, which, with slight amendments, was adopted by the Convention in the following form:—

"We, the peoples of the United Nations, determined to save succeeding generations from the scourge of war, which twice in our lifetime has brought untold sorrow to mankind, and

to reaffirm faith in fundamental human rights, in the dignity and value of the human person, in the equal rights of men and women and of nations large and small, and

to establish conditions under which justice and respect for the obligations arising from treaties and other sources of international law can be maintained, and

to promote social progress and better standards of life in larger freedom,

and for these ends

to practise tolerance and live together in peace with one another as good neighbours, and

to unite our strength to maintain international peace and security, and

by the accepting of principles and the institution of methods to insure that armed force shall not be used, save in the common interest, and

to employ international machinery for the promotion of economic and social advancement of all peoples have resolved to combine our efforts to accomplish these aims.

Accordingly, our respective Governments, through representatives assembled in the City of San Francisco, who have exhibited their full powers found to be in good and due form, have agreed to the present charter of the United Nations and do hereby establish an international organization to be known as the United Nations."

On May 1 he presided over a plenary session of the Convention in which he urged strongly that the five Great Powers' unanimity for taking action was essential; and by the calm force of his wisdom prevented a breaking up of the proceedings on this crucial question.

Not content with his arduous labours at San Francisco, at their conclusion this gallant young man of 75 found time and energy to address the Canadian Club at Ottawa. In this address he spoke on his favourite theme that "the human soul is not in the long run satisfied with material goods. Man cannot live by bread and comfort alone. . . . If he has no right sense of ultimate values, he will (as the Nazis did) create false debased values, which always end in brute force. At heart our human problem is this issue of ultimate values, of ultimate beliefs, of religion, the recession or decay of which has been, and may be again, the precursor of untold misfortunes to mankind." On 2 July he flew to London; had a great reception from South African returned prisoners of war at Brighton; visited the South African troops still in Italy and Egypt and finally arrived at Pretoria on 16 July. During his three and a half months' absence he had flown 29,000 miles and, when not in the air, had been working unceasingly. Small wonder that his South Africans gave him the greatest homecoming welcome accorded to any South African, as he made his triumphal progress through Pretoria's crowded streets, lined with troops and with an aerial escort, to the Union buildings. He himself said at San Francisco that this was "the last battle of the old war-horse"—*credat Judæus.*

(3) SMUTS AT HOME

We have seen in an earlier chapter how closely Jan Smuts and Sibella Krige—Jannie and Isie as they were known to their closest friends—were bound together, almost from childhood, by common interests and enthusiasms—an intimacy hardly interrupted by Smuts's absence at Cambridge and the English bar, and in May, 1897, when he was finding his feet at the Johannesburg bar, crowned by their happy marriage.[9] But by that time the storm was gathering which for over two years was to

[9] See above, Chapter 2.

part husband and wife. After the occupation of Pretoria by Roberts in the middle of 1900 the Boer Government had been dispersed, and Smuts began his apprenticeship for the guerilla warfare which eventually brought him through the Free State and Cape Colony almost up to its north-western border.

At first Mrs. Smuts stayed on at Pretoria, where their little son, their only child so far, died. Later she was deported by the British to Pietermaritzburg in Natal. Not only did she never see her husband during these two years, but received no letters from him, only stray rumours, generally to the effect that he had been killed. While in Natal she was anxious to help the other mothers and give some teaching to the children in the concentration camps, but was not allowed to do any teaching; and she suffered all the more in her enforced idleness, under her bereavement by the little son's death, by her anxiety about her husband's fate, and from her grief and horror at the deaths of many thousand women and children in the concentration camps.

After the treaty of Vereeniging, Smuts and his wife returned to Pretoria, he to resume his practice at the bar, and both at first embittered by the results of the peace and the grievances they felt against the Milner regime. She, even more than her husband, lived a very quiet life here, quite independent of society of any kind, busying herself chiefly with her new babies, her books and her household affairs. At that time she seldom wrote even to well-tried friends in England, such as Miss Hobhouse, who had exposed the evils of the concentration camps, but if any such came to see her she always had a warm welcome for them. She fully shared the views expressed by her husband in a letter to Miss Hobhouse which was published in England,[10] and on one occasion created quite a flutter in government circles by appearing in the Pretoria Zoological Gardens with a Vierkleur flag as a kerchief draped across her breast.

[10] See above, Chapter 4.

But when, in May, 1904, Botha founded *Het Volk*,[11] not only to reconcile the so-called *Hands-uppers* who had fallen by the way with the more stalwart *Bitter-enders*, but also to give voice to the needs of the Boer people, not in opposition to, but in co-operation with the English section of the community, she, with her husband, threw herself enthusiastically into the movement. Thereafter, always in close unity with him, she entered more and more into the greatness of his work in building up co-operation between those who, in the past, had fought each other. Under her leadership a band of women colleagues went about the country with her, travelling on arduous journeys, arousing and organizing the interest of women in the cause. Her organizing powers at elections were put to even more important use during the last and the present wars. She has always loved young people, so it was natural that the fighting forces of South Africa stirred her deepest sympathy. In both wars, especially in this one, she has been foremost in arranging from home for their support in every way that her quick understanding prompted; gifts and comforts in well thought out detail have been sent under her inspiration to every front where South African soldiers, English- or Afrikaans-speaking, as well as native and coloured auxiliaries, are to be found. In this connexion Smuts himself, hard worker as he is, has often said that he could never have done what she has accomplished.

At home Smuts and his wife have been blessed with three daughters and three more sons to succeed the son they lost in those three bitter years of the Boer War—Santa, married to Mr. Weyers, the manager of Smuts's home farm, who has three children; Katerina Prunella (Cato) who married Bancroft Clark of Street, Somerset; Jacob Daniel, "Jappie," born 1906, now married with four daughters; Sylma, who married an English South African; Jannie Christiaan, born 1912, married to an English South African girl; Louis Annie (named after Botha and his wife), born 1914, now a qualified doctor

11 See above, Chapter 4.

and married to an Ulsterman. When their father came back in 1919 after his long absence in German East Africa, in England and the continent, the two youngest children barely knew him, while the eldest thought he should not have signed the Treaty of Versailles.[12] At any rate it looks as if the Jannie and Sibella Smuts stock is not likely to be soon extinguished.

When in office, during the parliamentary session, Smuts lives at Grote Schoor in the Cape peninsula, left by Rhodes to the prime minister of the Union he foresaw: but, beautiful as its house and grounds are, it is inconvenient in many ways and expensive to keep up. Smuts's real home is at Irene, the next station to Pretoria on the railway to Johannesburg. Originally bought in a somewhat ramshackle condition shortly after the Boer War, it was then quite small, but has gradually been enlarged, somewhat at haphazard, to meet the needs of a growing family. It is still a modest, typically Boer house, with its wide stoep, the chief meeting-place of the family and of his numerous visitors.

Like Botha, too, Smuts has aspirations to be a farmer. He cultivates, with the help of a manager, the farm comprised in his Irene property and keeps there a prize bull and pedigree cattle. He also owns a back-veld farm, seventy miles north of Pretoria, where he has a herd of Afrikaner cattle for trek-work; and, considering his other manifold activities as statesman, philosopher and writer, he has proved successful even in that field.

In their hospitable home at Irene, both Smuts and his wife are only too glad to welcome their numerous visitors from all parts of the world; and fortunate are those invited to stay for the family tea, presided over by Mrs. Smuts, where the general talk is unrestrained and always interesting. Specially favoured guests are then sometimes invited to a private talk with the master himself in his vast library, his special sanctum and the most notable room in the

12 Mrs. Millin, *op. cit.*, 70.

house.[13] Smuts's library contains the books he needs for his almost encyclopædic interests—books on philosophy, religion, science in all its branches, history—political and constitutional—memoirs, military strategy and tactics, poetry. He himself is a voracious reader, able, even in the times of the greatest political or military crises, to throw off for the moment the affairs of state to master some new book on an apparently extraneous topic. In the black December of 1939, for example, he remarked casually to a friend: "I've been reading two new books about Jesus, by a Frenchman and a Jew."[14] In reality such a confession may not be so paradoxical as it at first sight appears: for after all the *primum mobile* for Smuts in all his hotly-contested wars has been to clear away tyrannies and shackles on the human spirit and get down to the really important business of peace, the abolition of tyranny and the growth of the human spirit. As he himself once said to an American friend during a night talk together in the Kruger Park: "I have but one merit, that of never despairing. I remain at heart an optimist";—an optimism which his friend attributed to "His bodily vigour, his power of work, the range and clarity of his mind, his delight in the fauna and flora of his own beloved native land, his immense interest in almost every phase of science . . . and his sure conviction that in this world Good is finally more powerful than Evil."[15]

---

[13] A delightful account of Smut's table-talk is given in B. K. Long's *In Smuts's Camp*, pp. 6-91.

[14] Mrs. Millin, 70.

[15] I. W. Lamont, "Smuts, World Leader in War and Peace," in *Saturday Review of Literature*, N.Y., 6 May, 1944.

I am deeply indebted to Mr. and Mrs. Gillett, friends of General Smuts for nearly a quarter of a century, for information in this and many other chapters.

Chapter 12

Botha and Smuts—*par nobile fratum*

THERE CAN be few, if any, parallels in history of such close co-operation between two statesmen, so utterly different in training, attainments and character, as that between Botha and Smuts. Richelieu and Father Joseph may at first sight come to mind; but in that instance, though there was close co-operation directed towards the same ultimate objects, the statesman and the subterranean worker were always strictly in the relation of master and servant. Botha and Smuts, on the other hand, are always rightly thought of as colleagues and the closest of friends, each having the same objects, and each contributing his own special characteristics to the furtherance of their common aims. Among our own statesmen, the close alliance of Cobden, the great thinker on free trade, and Bright, the great orator of the movement, may be a closer parallel to the great South African pair.

Both South African statesmen took a leading part in persuading their people to agree to the treaty of Vereeniging, not because they liked it, but because they realized that it was the only means left for preserving them as a people at all. Having accomplished this as the first step to resurgence—for a time, but only for a brief time, the two took different lines. Botha forthwith set himself to revive the spirit of his Boer fellow-countrymen, constituting himself their natural leader and adviser in all their difficulties, pressing their claims on the Milner government, and setting them an example of good husbandry in giving up his ruined farm at Vryheid and gradually building up a new model farm with first-class stock and up-to-date equipment at Standerton. Smuts, perhaps for the only time in his life, gave way to despair and bitterness of spirit, but this phase lasted only until, in 1904, Botha started organizing *Het Volk* to express the grievances and aspirations of his people and so to exert pressure on the British government. Smuts at once joined the new organisation with enthusiasm; and forthwith became one of its main leaders after Botha. Then, on the formation of the Campbell Bannerman government, he went, with Botha's blessing, to England to press his country's claims to have a voice in their own affairs, and was doubtless largely instrumental in persuading the prime minister to make his wise and magnificent gesture, to confer the franchise on those who only four years before had been England's enemies in the field.

From this time forward Botha and Smuts became the almost undisputed leaders of South Africa, bound together not merely by patriotic aims but also by the closest personal affection. In this happy combination Botha, *Oubaas* —the old chief—was the man of poise and sober judgment, Smuts the brilliant adventurer, *onze Jannie,* the *Klein Baas,* as he was called by the chief for whom he had an almost filial love. It was they who, after the brief period of responsible government in the Transvaal and the Free State, were the leading spirits in settling the form of Union adopted by the four South African colonies. They also were the only two ministers who counted in the first two Union ministries until the death of Botha in 1919. No two men could have been better complements to one another. Botha was one of those rare men who appear, and are, solid as a rock. Not clever, nor, as a rule, quick in arriving at his decisions, more sensitive than Smuts to opposition, he had his occasional fits of depression: but when, after discussions with his fellow-countrymen, sometimes carried on to inordinate length, he had once made up his mind, he was immovable in abiding by the decision he had come to. Smuts, on the other hand, impatient of long discussions and relying mainly on the cabinet of his own mind, often came to his decisions secretly and rapidly, much to the disturbance of his slow-thinking fellow-Boers and sometimes even of the more agile-minded English section. Instances of such surprise decisions may be found in his secret deportation of labour leaders after the riots and strike in Johannesburg in 1914, and his own secret and risky journey to the same city to deal, personally and unguarded, with the even more serious riots in 1922.[1]

Of the two, Botha was less an object of violent attack from his own Boer nationals than Smuts. Always more accessible to the common man, a farmer himself, as were most of his own countrymen, and so easily understanding their difficulties, Botha was always willing to talk with them on topics with which they were familiar, as the old President, Kruger, used to do on his stoep. But even he had his moments of depression, especially in the last few years of his life, when he was left alone without his beloved Jannie, then in England, to help him, and when he was laid low by his growing illness and had increasing difficulties with his own countrymen. But even then, as appears in Lord Buxton's loving appreciation of him, he still had brave powers of resilience. Happily in the last years of his life he was able to rejoin Smuts at Versailles and to persuade him to agree to the treaty, though both of them disagreed with some of its provisions, so that the League of Nations clauses, so dear to them both, might be preserved. Even his opponents could assent to Smuts's touching words at his burial: "the greatest, cleanest, sweetest soul of all my days." To us in this country he must always appear as one of the great bulwarks of our safety by his staunch adherence to the oath he had taken at Vereeniging and to the debt he owed us in returning to our Boer fellow-citizens of the Empire the practical independence they had lost in the Boer War.

Smuts is a far more complicated character. He is not only a statesman and a successful soldier in war, but also a notable student and philosopher, with a complete theory of the universe of his own. Indeed, one might call him one of the most all-embracing geniuses of our age. This very diversity of interests has made him suspect to many, both here and in South Africa, who cannot believe that such a comprehension of so many interests does not conceal some hidden flaw. But in his variegated career he has always, when the need has appeared, put first things first. As a

---

[1] See above, Chapters 5 and 8.

soldier in the Boer War, and in German West and East Africa he was absorbed in military needs and strategy to the temporary exclusion of all his other interests. As a statesman in South African politics before the Boer War and as minister after the war, his only rival to pre-eminence was his friend Botha, during Botha's too short-lived career. Nor has his statecraft been limited to South Africa. During the last war he took a notable part in British and continental politics and administration, and he has been one of the foremost advocates of the League of Nations, which owed much to his enthusiastic initiative and support, both at its inception at Versailles and since then by heartening addresses delivered in Europe, America and South Africa. In this present war he has still shown himself pregnant of wise counsels for the rehabilitation of a shattered world. In his politics he has never been static, especially in his growing appreciation of the need for developing and encouraging better treatment of the native races and for giving them more direct control of their own affairs. As an athlete he has long been known as a formidable mountaineer on the by no means negligible mountains of South Africa. Last, but not least, he has a philosophy of life and the universe expounded in his eloquent and attractive volume on *Holism*.

How far does this almost universal genius of his carry conviction, it may be asked. To be entirely popular he has perhaps spread himself too much. No one section of the populations he has addressed in person or through his books feels inclined to award him the highest palm, for there is always an instinctive distrust of the universal genius. Nevertheless there can be no question but that he is one of the most vital and effective personalities of his age, whether as statesman, soldier or thinker. How far is he popular? In this country immensely so, by his understanding of our way of life, of our politics and of our literature, and his readiness to express his sincere admiration of the characteristics of which we are most proud. As to his popularity in his own country I once asked one of his dearest friends if the remark of one of his biographers that he was "the idol of the army" was true. "No," was the reply, "hardly that: he is respected, but hardly popular," a verdict which would probably satisfy Smuts himself. Today, however, the wonderful enthusiasm with which *Oubaas* (as he is now in turn called) was acclaimed by the gigantic gathering of all sections of the South African community, on his return from San Francisco in July, 1945, indicates that he has attained popularity as well as profound respect.

To both these great men may be applied that brave Boer motto:

Alles zal recht kom.

Bibliography

The following books and pamphlets have been found to be useful materials for this book.

Annual Register (various dates).

H. C. Armstrong, *Grey Steel* (*i.e.*, J. C. Smuts), 1937.

Lord Buxton, *General Botha*, 1924.

A. F. Campbell, *Smuts and the Swastika*, 1942. *General Smuts*, 1943.

J. J. Collyer, *The Africans with General Smuts in German East Africa*, 1939.

F. S. Crafford, *Jan Smuts*, 1944.

J. H. V. Crowe, *General Smuts's Campaign in East Africa*, 1918

P. V. Engelengberg, *General Louis Botha*, 1929.

J. H. Hofmeyr, *South Africa*.

R. H. Kiernan, *General Smuts*, 1943.

J. W. Lamont, "Smuts: World Leader in War and Peace," in *Saturday Review of Literature*, N.Y., May, 1944.

N. Levis, *Jan Smuts*, 1917.

D. Lloyd George, *War Memoirs* (v.d.)

B. K. Long, *In Smuts's Camp*, 1945.

Sir Chas. Lucas, *The Empire at War*, Vol. 4, 1925.

S. G. Millin, *General Smuts*, 2 Vols.; *World Black-out*, 1944. *The Reeling Earth*, 1945.

L. E. Neame, *General Hertzog*, 1930.

Official History of the Great War; East Africa I, 1941.

Race Relations News, a monthly bulletin on native questions.

D. Reitz, *On Commando, Trekking On, No Outspan* (v.d.)

E. W. Smith, *Aggrey of Africa, A Study in Black and White*, 1929. (Useful for native questions).

H. Spender, *General Botha.*

J. C. Smuts, *Holism and Evolution,* 1926. Reviewed in:—*Journal of Philosophic Studies,* 1927. *Nature,* 1927. *International Journal of Ethics,* 1926-27.

Addresses by Gen. Smuts:
 Africa and some World problems, 1930.
 Freedom, 1934. And many others.

South African House of Assembly Debates.

Von Lettow Vorbeck, *My Reminiscences in E. Africa,* 1920.

South African Outlook. (Useful for native questions).

South Africa, weekly journal published in London.

E. Walker, *The British Empire.*

Sir E. Walton, *Inner History of National Convention of South Africa,* 1912.

Basil Williams, *Cecil Rhodes;* Articles on *Botha* in *D.N.B.; South Africa* in *Encycl. Brit.*

I have also been much helped by information given in talks and letters of the late Deneys Reitz, S. E. Coetzee at South Africa House, and many others.

Afterword

Basil Williams's biography of two statesmen and the founding of their nation encompasses the full life of the one (Botha, who died in 1919) and all but the last five years of that of Jan Christian Smuts, who died in 1950. All of the great events of his career are included; only his continuing service in the United Nations to 1947 runs beyond its scope.

Smuts's domestic career ended when his government was again defeated by the Nationalists in 1948 and he announced his retirement. He died near Pretoria on September 11, 1950.

The book ends on the note of high optimism that came with the close of World War II. But before Smuts died, his South Africa was facing deeper internal crises than he ever anticipated. His life had been given to healing the split between two European communities, the Dutch and the British. But the rift between European and African, always in the background—and discussed in the book in terms of Smuts's own approach to "native problems"—erupted with a force that shook not only the Union itself but a world which was witnessing most of old colonial Africa attaining independent nationhood while South Africa attempted to stem the tide by suppression and apartheid.

Botha and Smuts spent their lives in the achievement of a unified nation. They were spared the conflict, unresolved today, that may yet destroy their work.

Index

Index